DATE DUE

DEMCO 38-296

Liberty
& LEARNING
MILTON FRIEDMAN'S VOUCHER IDEA
AT FIFTY

R

Liberty
& LEARNING
MILTON FRIEDMAN'S VOUCHER IDEA
AT FIFTY

EDITED BY ROBERT C. ENLOW AND LENORE T. EALY

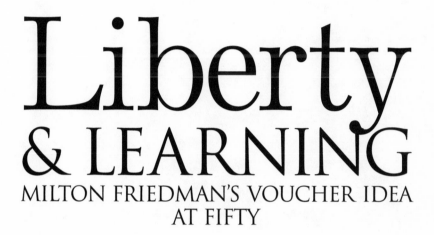

CATO
INSTITUTE
WASHINGTON, D.C.

Library of Congress Cataloging-in-Publication Data

Liberty & learning : Milton Friedman's voucher idea at fifty / Robert C.
Enlow, Lenore T. Ealy
    p. cm.
    Includes bibliographical references and index.
    ISBN 1-930865-93-7 (cloth : alk. paper) -- ISBN 1-930865-86-4 (paper :
alk. paper)
    1. Educational vouchers--United States. 2. Friedman, Milton, 1912-
I. Enlow, Robert C. II. Ealy, Lenore T. III. Title: Liberty and learning.

LB2825.L33 2006
379.1'110973--dc22   2006049573

Cover design by Jon Meyers.
Printed in the United States of America.

CATO INSTITUTE
1000 Massachusetts Ave., N.W.
Washington, D.C. 20001
www.cato.org

Contents

PROLOGUE: A Personal Retrospective
Milton Friedman   vii

INTRODUCTION
Robert C. Enlow and Lenore T. Ealy   1

1. The Role of Government in Education: Enduring
   Principles, New Circumstances, and the Question of
   "Shelf Life"
   Guilbert C. Hentschke   11

2. Choice, Religion, Community, and Educational Quality
   John E. Brandl   25

3. A Culture of Choice
   Abigail Thernstrom   35

4. Milton Friedman, Vouchers, and Civic Values
   Jay P. Greene   49

5. Give Us Liberty and Give Us Depth
   John E. Coons   57

6. Is There Hope for Expanded School Choice?
   Eric A. Hanushek   67

7. Free-Market Strategy and Tactics in K–12 Education
   Myron Lieberman   81

8. A Critique of Pure Friedman: An Empirical
   Reassessment of "The Role of Government in
   Education"
   Andrew Coulson   103

9. Discipline Is the Key to Milton Friedman's Gold
   Standard for Education Reform
   John Merrifield   125

10. From Universal to Targeted Vouchers: The Relevance
    of the Friedmans' Proposals for Developing Countries
    James Tooley   139

EPILOGUE: School Vouchers Turn 50, But the Fight Is
Just Beginning
Milton Friedman   155

ABOUT THE CONTRIBUTORS   159

ABOUT THE EDITORS   165

INDEX   167

Prologue: A Personal Retrospective

Milton Friedman

Little did I know when I published an article in 1955 on "The Role of Government in Education" that it would lead to my becoming an activist for a major reform in the organization of schooling, and indeed that my wife and I would be led to establish a foundation to promote parental choice. The original article was not a reaction to a perceived deficiency in schooling. The quality of schooling in the United States then was far better than it is now, and both my wife and I were satisfied with the public schools we had attended. My interest was in the philosophy of a free society. Education was the area that I happened to write on early. I then went on to consider other areas as well. The end result was *Capitalism and Freedom*, published seven years later with the education article as one chapter.

With respect to education, I pointed out that government was playing three major roles: (1) legislating compulsory schooling, (2) financing schooling, and (3) administering schools. I concluded that there was some justification for compulsory schooling and the financing of schooling, but "the actual administration of educational institutions by the government, the 'nationalization,' as it were, of the bulk of the 'education industry' is much more difficult to justify on free-market or, so far as I can see, on any other grounds." Yet finance and administration "could readily be separated. Governments could require a minimum of schooling financed by giving the parents vouchers redeemable for a given sum per child per year to be spent on purely educational services. . . . Denationalizing schooling," I went on, "would widen the range of choice available to parents. . . . If present public expenditure were made available to parents regardless of where they send their children, a wide variety

---

A slightly different version of this essay appeared in the *Wall Street Journal* on June 9, 2005, under the headline "Free to Choose" as well as in the *School Choice Advocate*, June 2005, under the title "A Personal Retrospective."

of schools would spring up to meet the demand. . . . Here, as in other fields, competitive enterprise is likely to be far more efficient in meeting consumer demand than either nationalized enterprises or enterprises run to serve other purposes."

Though the article, and then *Capitalism and Freedom*, generated some academic and popular attention at the time, so far as we know no attempts were made to introduce a system of educational vouchers until the Nixon administration, when the Office of Economic Opportunity took up the idea and offered to finance actual experiments. One result of that initiative was an ambitious attempt to introduce vouchers in the large cities of New Hampshire, which appeared to be headed for success until it was aborted by the opposition of the teachers' unions and the educational administrators— one of the first instances of the oppositional role they were destined to play in subsequent decades. Another result was an experiment in the Alum Rock school system involving a choice of schools within a public system.

What really led to increased interest in vouchers was the deterioration of schooling, dating in particular from 1965 when the National Education Association converted itself from a professional association to a trade union. Concern about the quality of education led to the establishment of the National Commission on Excellence in Education, whose final report "A Nation at Risk" was published in 1983. It used the following quote from Paul Copperman to dramatize its own conclusion:

> Each generation of Americans has outstripped its parents in education, in literacy, and in economic attainment. For the first time in the history of our country, the educational skills of one generation will not surpass, will not equal, will not even approach, those of their parents.

"A Nation at Risk" stimulated much soul-searching and a whole series of major attempts to reform the government educational system. Those reforms, however extensive or bold, have, it is widely agreed, had a negligible effect on the quality of the public school system. Though spending per pupil has more than doubled since 1970, after allowing for inflation, students continue to rank low in international comparisons, dropout rates are high, and scores on SATs and the like have fallen and remain flat. Simple literacy, let alone functional literacy, in the United States is almost surely lower at the beginning of the 21st century than it was a century earlier. And all this is despite a major increase in real spending per student since "A Nation at Risk" was published.

One result has been experimentation with such alternatives as vouchers, tax credits, and charter schools. Government voucher programs are in effect in a few places (Wisconsin, Ohio, Florida, the District of Columbia); private voucher programs are widespread; tax credits for educational expenses have been adopted in at least three states; and tax credit vouchers (tax credits for gifts to scholarship-granting organizations) have been adopted in three states. In addition, a major legal obstacle to the adoption of vouchers was removed when the Supreme Court affirmed the legality of the Cleveland voucher program in 2002. However, all of those programs are limited; taken together, they cover only a small fraction of all children in the country.

Throughout this long period, we have been repeatedly frustrated by the gulf between the clear and present need, the burning desire of parents to have more control over the schooling of their children, on the one hand, and the adamant and effective opposition of trade union leaders and educational administrators to any change that would in any way reduce their control of the educational system.

We have been involved in two initiatives in California to enact a statewide voucher system (in 1993 and 2000). In both cases, the initiatives were carefully drawn up and the voucher sums moderate. In both cases, nine months or so before the election, public opinion polls recorded a sizable majority in favor of the initiative. In addition, of course, there was a sizable group of fervent supporters, whose hopes of finally getting control of their children's schooling ran high. In each case, about six months before the election, opponents of vouchers launched a well-financed and thoroughly unscrupulous campaign against the initiative. Television ads blared that vouchers would break the budget, whereas in fact they would reduce spending since the proposed voucher was to be only a fraction of what government was spending per student. Teachers were induced to send home with their students misleading propaganda against the initiative. Dirty tricks of every variety were financed from a very deep purse. The result was to convert the initial majority into a landslide defeat. That has also occurred in Washington State, Colorado, and

Michigan. Opposition like this explains why progress has been so slow in such a good cause.

The good news is that, despite the setbacks, public interest in and support for vouchers and tax credits continues to grow. Legislative proposals to channel government funds directly to students rather than to schools are under consideration in something like 20 states. Sooner or later there will be a breakthrough; we shall get a universal voucher plan in one or more states. When we do, a competitive private educational market serving parents who are free to choose the school they believe best for each child will demonstrate how it can revolutionize schooling.

Introduction

Robert C. Enlow and Lenore T. Ealy

In 1955 Milton Friedman published an essay, "The Role of Government in Education," that articulated an old idea of liberty in a fresh way. The centerpiece of that essay was a proposal to improve learning in elementary and secondary schools by separating the government financing of education from the government administration of schools.

That proposal, which launched the modern school choice movement, was a radical departure from the prevailing ideology of the time. It ran counter to the growing power of the teachers' unions and presented a vision of parental liberty and responsibility at odds with the educational establishment, which was putting the final touches on centralizing the systems that taxed and operated schools and institutionalizing the educational theories of John Dewey and others.

In the 50 years since Friedman posed the idea, educational choice has been a hotly debated topic. The idea and the policy proposals it has generated have been criticized on many levels, and supporters of educational choice have run headlong into a long-term battle against a well-funded educational establishment with a vested interest in maintaining the status quo. Meanwhile, much has changed in education and society since 1955. Dissatisfaction with school performance has grown, ambitious efforts to reform education have met with little success, and American schools have been largely unable to respond to economic and technological forces that demand new cognitive and technical skills from the next generation of citizens.

It is in this context that we decided the time was right for a critical reassessment of the progress and prospects of educational choice as the key ingredient of meaningful educational reform. We wondered whether Milton Friedman's 50-year-old vision of educational liberty was still relevant in today's society, and if it is, why it hadn't swept like wildfire across America. To help us answer those questions, we

1

approached some of the nation's top experts on educational reform and asked them to reexamine the 1955 essay with the following question in mind: "Do Milton and Rose Friedman's ideas on school reform have merit for the 21st century?"

Our aim in this endeavor was not merely to produce a celebratory volume in which the contributors congratulated themselves for believing in the principles of educational choice espoused by the Friedmans. Rather, it was our intention to seek broad input from a variety of thinkers—some who agree with the Friedmans and some who don't, some who are academicians and some who are practitioners. The goal was to create an open and honest dialogue that enhances our understanding of both liberty and learning.

As one would imagine, the contributors to this volume took a variety of approaches to the question posed. Some authors examined the question from a theoretical position; others took a very pragmatic approach. Some affirm Friedman's position; others raise questions. Some point to successful examples of educational choice policies; others question whether supporters of educational choice are headed in the right direction. Taken together, these thought-provoking essays are a compelling affirmation that Friedman's concept of educational choice has withstood the test of time.

* * * * *

Our examination of Friedman's voucher idea begins with an essay by Guilbert Hentschke, a lifelong educator and former dean of the School of Education at the University of Southern California. Hentschke investigates the shelf life of the idea by examining the "changes in circumstances and conditions" surrounding the roles of education, households, and government in our society since 1955. This is a useful way to begin our considerations, for, as Hentschke observes, the changes over the past half century have been quite dramatic in many areas. We are moving rapidly from an industrial economy to a knowledge economy, "where the education of individuals is much more directly associated with their well-being and by inference with the well-being of communities and countries where they reside." Hentschke proposes that implementation of any voucher idea as public policy must take account of present circumstances in education, households (and the neighborhoods in which they are located), and government.

Hentschke thus provides a helpful backdrop for considering the remaining essays, which we have ordered around three themes: essays that address ongoing concerns about choice and democratic values, essays that primarily examine technical principles of proposed voucher policies, and an essay that begins to direct our vision forward to see how expanded parental choice in education might play out in practice, both in the United States and globally.

Educational Choice and Democratic Values

The contributions from John Brandl, Abigail Thernstrom, Jay Greene, and John Coons encourage us to view educational choice as part of an ongoing civic dialogue about democratic values and their expression through social institutions.

By invoking the thought of John Dewey as a frame for his essay, Brandl takes us into the heart of this dialogue as it shaped the development of education policy in America throughout the 20th century. While acknowledging the almost metaphysical regard Dewey had for schools as the purveyors of America's secular religion of democracy, Brandl suggests that Dewey's longest-lasting influence should be his ultimate pragmatism. Dewey's own primary injunction to find what works, Brandl argues, makes it increasingly difficult to produce a positive case for public schools when research makes clear that there is little correlation between public spending and educational outcomes.

Rather than accepting at face value, however, Friedman's economic faith that private schools emerging to serve consumers in an educational marketplace would provide a better mechanism for aligning spending and results in education, Brandl asks us to consider whether a complementary "communitarian" rationale for educational choice can also be discovered. Examining the ongoing comparative success of sectarian schools in aligning spending and results as well as in diminishing the differentials arising from family characteristics, Brandl suggests that "perhaps it is not the discipline of competition but the inspiration of community that is the central explanation for the efficacy of choice."

In the following essay, Abigail Thernstrom echoes Brandl's concern about the sizable differences in educational attainment among American children, but she does not believe that the issue is fundamentally one of socioeconomics. Rather, Thernstrom points us to

3

the "troubling racial gap" in American education and observes that "black and Hispanic students, whether their families are affluent or low income, are typically far behind whites and Asians, and part of the problem is their disconnect from mainstream American values." Because Latin American immigrants typically follow a more hopeful pattern, with each generation moving somewhat up the ladders of economic, social, and educational attainment, Thernstrom is particularly concerned with the plight of black children in America. She argues that the dismal failure of desegregation measures and antipoverty programs at equalizing educational and economic opportunity for blacks in America requires us to look more deeply at pervasive cultural issues. Thernstrom's appeal is for us to consider that the very cultural attitudes and habits that accompany the freedom to choose—as they shape public policy, families, schools, and most essentially the horizons of individuation and possibility experienced by students themselves—become essential to meaningful educational reform.

Jay Greene's contribution complements those of Brandl and Thernstrom by examining what Friedman's 1955 essay really had to say about such issues as the role of religious schools as well as the implications of vouchers for desegregation. Greene asserts that Friedman was deeply interested in the possible impact of school choice on religious schooling and desegregation. He points us to a growing body of research that is emerging to suggest that universal implementation of vouchers would enhance political tolerance and reduce school segregation, thus bearing out Friedman's predictions about the potentially benign impact of school choice on civic values. He also takes Amy Gutmann and others to task for misinterpreting Friedman's concern for civic values, ultimately arguing that "it is difficult to see how anyone could actually read his 1955 article and come away with the idea that Friedman was unconcerned with the effects of education on civic values or that he was conceding that vouchers would cause segregation." Greene concludes that Friedman's theoretical case for educational choice has stood the test of time and remains a most hopeful approach not only for increasing the educational attainment of students but also for enhancing democratic stability.

The essay by John Coons completes this section by raising questions about the limits of the rhetoric of liberty and autonomy. "Certainly Friedman has been right all along," Coons tells us, "to suppose that America needs to subsidize parental choice and to remake schooling into a market that includes all players. It puzzles, then, that his form of the message has proved so unwelcome among a public otherwise enthusiastic for tales of Adam Smith." Coons proposes that one reason for the failure of choice to receive broader political support has been the overreliance of supporters of vouchers on the rhetorical language of liberty. Holding freedom as the ultimate value in the debate has allowed for the confusion of the end goal of the eventual autonomy of the child with the present responsibility of parents. Such confusion of ends and means has given ammunition to advocates of government schooling who can justify their position on the assumption that common folks cannot exercise choice well. In Coons's opinion, this emboldens opponents of school choice to make the counterintuitive claim that "America's disenfranchisement of have-not families at least works to the long-range benefit of their children." Coons would open the dialogue about the role of education in a free society to include a deeper discussion of the integrity of the family as a "bedrock social good." According to Coons, the argument for choice is not ultimately persuasive using the language of liberty alone; it could be made stronger by recognizing the "powerful, authoritative guiding institution" of the family, rather than children alone, as the focus of our educational policy and practice.

From Here to There

The second group of essays by Eric Hanushek, Myron Lieberman, Andrew Coulson, and John Merrifield affirms the basic tenets of educational choice but takes us deeper into the continuing controversies and challenges that surround efforts to implement Friedman-style voucher programs.

Eric Hanushek describes the problem of implementing educational choice in relation to the historical trend toward increasing centralization of decisionmaking in education over the last century, a trend that has moved decisions away from parents and local administrators and toward state bureaucracies. This move, suggests Hanushek, has reduced the sphere of parental decisionmaking primarily to decisions about where to live. To extend Hanushek's observations, we would note that despite the beginnings of devolution in other areas where centralization has proven unworkable, it is arguable that, with the No Child Left Behind Act and the present willingness in Washington to spend political capital on education reform, the trend in education decisionmaking continues to move toward the center.

Against this backdrop, Hanushek cites Friedman's voucher proposal as "the best vehicle for balancing legitimate state interests and the natural interests of families." Unfortunately, Hanushek observes, in light of the opposition from teachers' unions, the voucher idea has met with little policy success. Nevertheless, he adds that progress in finding new ways for families to express their interests in and make choices about the education of their children has occurred, particularly in the areas of homeschooling, intradistrict open enrollment, interdistrict open enrollment, and most notably the charter school movement. All of those advances coupled with the growing recognition that American schools are "extraordinarily expensive but not very effective" will pave the way, Hanushek suggests, for experimentation with purer forms of choice in the future.

Myron Lieberman is not so optimistic and calls upon supporters of educational choice to recognize their failure to understand the essence of educational free markets and engage in the inevitable battle that must be won against the teachers' unions. Rather than divert our attention to cultural arguments about the values inherent in school choice and the rhetoric most likely to persuade in the public and political realm, Lieberman urges us to look again more deeply at the economic theory of the benefits of competition that Friedman brought to bear on the question. A voucher is not always a voucher. Even the best voucher trials conducted to date have failed to foster the optimum conditions in which vouchers could truly help elicit market-driven discovery and innovation in schooling. Lieberman believes that true advocates of educational choice must resist the temptation to tinker any longer at the margins with half-formulated voucher programs that may be passable but are not really workable or anything like the kind of educational marketplace envisaged by Milton Friedman. What our schools need instead is to be situated in an industry that is not incrementally changed but revolutionized so that it can continually undergo the process of "creative destruction" that incentivizes and funds research and development through the competitive process.

In the next essay, Andrew Coulson reaches a conclusion similar to Lieberman's: that advocates of vouchers must pay closer heed to the critical principles Friedman articulated in introducing the case for educational vouchers. While Lieberman wants to reclaim an accurate understanding of market competition, Coulson seeks to make an even purer case for limiting government involvement in education across the board. Recalling Friedman's affirmation that direct payment of tuition by parents is the ideal, Coulson asks what the best steps are to restore parental responsibility and capacity for consuming education at desirable levels. Bringing current empirical evidence to bear, Coulson finds little reason to presume that Americans have not been or would fail to be active consumers of education "in the absence of government intervention or heavy government subsidization." Coulson focuses our attention on the problem of third-party payer systems and asks how we can most effectively and with the least systemic distortion utilize third-party subsidies (whether through taxation or through voluntary private means) to ensure that "all families can afford to consume sufficient schooling of sufficiently high quality."

John Merrifield's essay rounds out this line of argument by acknowledging Friedman's proposal as the "Gold Standard" for education reform and by recognizing along with Coulson that Friedman's vision was of a transformation of schooling that would go beyond privatization of provision to privatization of funding. Merrifield can foresee an ultimate separation of school and state and thus implicitly draws a line in the sand between Friedman and John Dewey and a host of other Progressive social theorists and educators for whom schools were an essential tool in the process of "social control." Drawing upon an older conception of education as the handmaiden of human freedom, Merrifield argues that schools must be subject "to the forces of discipline and innovation that prevail where free enterprise operates." As Merrifield sees it, the challenge for advocates of freedom in general and educational freedom in particular is to leave compromise to politicians and refuse to settle for limited voucher initiatives that fail to allow full play for entrepreneurial discovery and participation.

Looking Forward

The final essay in our collection by James Tooley stands apart somewhat from the others and extends our consideration of the prospects of market-based education by examining the implications of Friedman's proposals in an international context. Tooley describes how Friedman's ideas inspired researchers such as E. G. West in Britain to deeper exploration of the history of education. West's findings later made it possible for Friedman to acknowledge that there was little evidence to justify compulsory schooling, the cornerstone of public funding for schooling.

Tooley's own research, growing out of the serendipitous discovery of a robust emerging tier of private schools in Hyderabad, India, has since begun to demonstrate that in developing countries as diverse as India, Ghana, China, and Kenya private schools for the poor are "mushrooming." This growing trend of entrepreneurs in the poorest communities of the world meeting the demand of poor families for access to quality education through fee-based private schools suggests that privatization of education is not the impossible dream or the nightmare of commercial rape that the opponents of vouchers proclaim. In fact, Tooley proposes that privatized education with targeted vouchers for the most disadvantaged is probably the most viable way to achieve education for all in developing countries.

This research has implications for America as well. Tooley and his colleagues are documenting how dedicated educators in the poorest of poor neighborhoods are building entrepreneurially successful schools that expand the educational opportunities of children and gain the confidence of parents more than do better-funded government schools. The fact that this can be achieved in such dire conditions should put to shame the entrenched anti-entrepreneurial prejudice of educational and policy leaders in the most developed nations. Tooley's research suggests that the abundant financial capital and robust market infrastructures in more-developed communities should be utilized to assist the development of an effective educational marketplace in less-developed communities. Far from corrupting education, the introduction of commercial incentives into education is clearly compatible both with improving service to the poorest among us and with cultivating greater respect for the decisionmaking abilities of most parents.

* * * * *

We hope that these essays, read individually and as a whole, will spark continued reflection and public discussion of questions at the heart of any free society: What are the sources of our freedom? What institutions are essential to instilling democratic values, and what role should those institutions play in encouraging the culture and habits of freedom? How do public policies best facilitate conditions of equal opportunity for all without establishing disincentives to discovery and innovation?

The condition and organization of education are critical components of the future freedom, security, and prosperity of every society. The more we infuse our educational institutions with the very practices that make us free, the more likely it is that we will pass on a legacy of freedom and responsibility to our children, thus ensuring a stable and democratic society now and forever.

Ultimately, the freedom of parents to take in and assess the information around them and the responsibility they bear to make the best educational decisions possible for their children must be at the heart of any truly free society. Those functions cannot be abdicated or delegated to government, or abrogated by it, without serious detriment to the habits of free people. We must recognize that more choice is simply better than less choice. As geographer Jack Sommer observes, "Choices . . . are not made from a finite list of predetermined items as if one were reading a menu at a restaurant; they are individual acts of creative construction which draw upon one's cognition of the material resources of the known world."[1]

Especially today, when the world is changing so rapidly around us because of the impact of technology and globalization on our societies, we must decentralize decisionmaking as much as possible to reap maximum social benefits from distributed local knowledge. And we must allow for the development of schools and educational programs that equip people to learn to observe the world around them, analyze the information they gather, and make informed personal decisions consonant with their own visions of human betterment and with the most worthy values of their communities. Sommer provides us a compelling conclusion:

> Choice and Liberty are the same, and as we seek to increase both we must be mindful that this can happen only by regarding the rights of others so that harm is avoided. Let no one think this is an easy task, nor one that should be taken lightly. The prospects for liberty in the 21st century continue to depend on how we confront this challenge.

That thought takes us back to Friedman's 1955 essay where he laid out his vision of the role of government in education. It was, and is, a vision that specifically limits government involvement in education to empowering parents to exercise educational freedom, and that leads directly to "a society that takes freedom of the individual, or more realistically the family, as its ultimate objective, and seeks to further this objective by relying primarily on voluntary exchange among individuals for the organization of economic activity."

In any such free society, there should be a constant dialogue about liberty and learning, and we offer this book as a contribution to that discussion.

Note

1. Jack Sommer, "Technology and Choice in a Shrinking World," Paper prepared for a Liberty Fund Colloquium, "Futurescapes: Prospecting for Liberty in the 21st Century," February 1990.

1. The Role of Government in Education: Enduring Principles, New Circumstances, and the Question of "Shelf Life"

Guilbert C. Hentschke

One of the stiffest tests that can be applied to any policy is the test of time. That is particularly true in the field of education where the half-life of most school reforms seems to be only a few years, after which they are rejected or "domesticated" beyond recognition. To seriously reexamine the idea of vouchers proposed by Milton Friedman fully half a century ago is to confront two issues simultaneously: the inherent merits of the idea and the inevitable changes in circumstances and conditions between then and now. It is a twofold test of the inherent worthiness of the idea and its "shelf life," or the degree to which it is more or less compelling today after 50 years of societal evolution. Because so much scholarly attention has already been directed to the merits of the proposal and its specific manifestations,[1] this essay focuses most of its attention on the second, or shelf-life, test.

In "The Role of Government in Education," Friedman constructed in 21 pages an argument on the appropriate roles of governments and families in the support for and provision of kindergarten through 12th grade (K–12) schooling, of which only several of the most fundamental features are summarized here. According to Friedman, government's primary role in a free economy is "to preserve the rules of the game by enforcing contracts, preventing coercion, and keeping markets free."[2] As a result, he concludes that families' educational prerogatives can be justifiably overridden by governments on only three bases: if education can be considered a "natural monopoly," if there are significant "neighborhood effects," or because of what he terms "paternalistic concern for children and other irresponsible individuals."[3]

11

Those issues, often ambiguously complex and substantially non-trivial, justify some but by no means all of the current involvement of government in education at both the compulsory and the postcompulsory levels. Based largely on the presumptions about education's neighborhood effects, arguments can be made for the state imposing minimum required levels of schooling and financing schooling. But it is difficult to see how neighborhood effects could justify the state's current involvement in "the actual administration of educational institutions by government."[4] In the same paper Friedman also argued against both the financing and the provision of strictly "vocational" education, because of its presumed lack of neighborhood effects, a somewhat separate topic addressed near the end of this essay.

Furthering his basic principles, Friedman posits that the case "that perhaps comes closest to being justified by these considerations ... is a mixed one under which governments would continue to administer some schools, but parents who chose to send their children to other schools would be paid a sum equal to the estimated cost of educating a child in a government school, provided that at least this sum was spent on education in an approved school."[5] "Let the subsidy be made available to parents regardless where they send their children—provided only that it be to schools that satisfy specified minimum standards."[6] Thus, Friedman introduces the modern concept of educational vouchers for K–12 schooling.

At the risk of ignoring important elaborations, qualifications, and conditions of Friedman's proposal, suffice it to say that the central argument was to shift significant portions of government education subsidies from providers on the supply side of schooling to households on the demand side. Suffice it also to say that many of the subsequent arguments about Friedman's proposal (both pro and con) hinged more on assumptions about the likely effects of voucher-like proposals and on the relative merits of specific initiatives than on a reanalysis of the fundamental proposition of the appropriate roles of government and households in schooling.[7]

Changes

Virtually all arguments about both—the proper *roles* for government and households as well as the likely *impacts* of specific voucher plans—include assumptions, assertions, and implications about the status and interactions of three topics: the nature of *education* itself, the proper role of *households* in pursuing education, and the proper role of *government* in fostering it. Assertions about those three topics form the three-legged stool of this analysis of Friedman's voucher proposal. Changes in those areas over half a century could well have changed the salience of Friedman's argument, prompting the question addressed in this essay: In what ways, if any, have changes over the last half century in education, households, and governments affected our views of and assumptions about vouchers and choice?

Changes in the Nature of Education

The nature of education has evolved in at least four ways over the last 50 years. First, education is a more consequential component of human well-being. We are now much further along the path toward a "knowledge economy" where the education of individuals is much more directly associated with their well-being and, by inference, with the well-being of the communities and countries where they reside.[8] Human capital and social capital have eclipsed physical capital as a manifestation of wealth and engine of wealth creation. What is between our ears is now much more important than how strong our backs are or whether we live near natural resources.

Second, different levels of education produce, as well as reflect, growing *differences* in earnings. The differences in payoffs for different levels of schooling are growing greater and greater, not shrinking.[9] Not only do higher levels of schooling have disproportionately higher payoffs, but higher levels of schooling are associated with greater opportunities for even more schooling. Schooling is at once the great equalizer, the key to future opportunity, and a key contributor to growing household economic inequality.

Third, what we used to consider a minimally "adequate" education is now much less than adequate. The minimally acceptable, "good enough," education bar has been raised significantly over 50 years. The "minimum level of schooling required to compete for improved life chances" is now clearly beyond what a typical high school education actually provides to its graduates.[10] Also, for many students, several years of "college" education are required to acquire the knowledge and skills that they should have been able to acquire in high school but, for whatever reasons, did not.[11]

13

Fourth, increases in early learning are more consequential than increases in later learning. We have come to understand over the last 50 years that increased learning at the "low" (early childhood) end of compulsory education has significant payoffs in school achievement, which raises the likelihood of individuals pursuing additional schooling and earning more as a result (private benefits), as well as payoffs in the form of subsequent public savings in remedial and special education, criminal justice, and welfare costs.[12] The neighborhood effects argument for early childhood development programs is reinforced by the disproportionately high economic returns derived from them. "Investments in high-quality early childhood development programs consistently generate benefit/cost ratios exceeding three to one, or more than a $3 return for every $1 invested, well above the one-to-one ratio needed to justify such investments."[13]

The arguments for extending public support of schooling beyond 12th grade are based on the same theories of investment in schooling, but the cost/benefit ratios of such investments are not likely to be nearly as robust. In both cases, the public and private benefits from increased schooling have grown significantly over the last half century.

Changes in the nature of education are, in effect, changes in the impact that education has on both the stock of human capital of households and the ability of governments to provide public goods, including education. Education is more important in our lives today because of its increased private *and* public returns, but changes in the nature of education affect households and governments differently.

Changes in Households

Households and their relation to education have changed during the last 50 years, in at least five interrelated ways. First, households recognize more than ever the significant and growing private returns to increased education and allocate increasing proportions of their disposable income to human capital development. During this period an entire "education industry" has come into prominence,[14] providing a wide range of "private-pay" educational goods and services, including educational toys (LeapPads), tutoring services (Educate), and whole schools (Nobel, Aspen Education Group). Private investments in education are increasing in an effort to capture some of the returns to enhanced learning.

Second, households, along with communities, are now widely recognized as major "educators" along with schools—both positively and negatively.[15] Both households and communities contribute significantly to the "social capital" available to children, and that influence on human capital development is at least as great as in the past and, if anything, growing stronger.[16] "Neighborhood effects" has taken on additional meaning. Higher levels of individual human capital positively affect our "neighbors," but we now also better appreciate how neighbors in turn influence both the social and human capital that each of us acquires.

Third, because parental income and education levels are now more highly correlated, those factors have significant direct and indirect influence on the educational levels of children. The educational wealth of families is thus becoming more of an asset transferable across generations, not unlike family economic wealth, although analysts differ on the degree and the weight of different contributing factors.[17]

Fourth, because inequalities in household income, wealth, and education levels are much greater today than half a century ago,[18] the contribution that households *can* make to the education of their children is becoming increasingly variable at the same time that it is becoming increasingly consequential. Predictably, the economic and social investments of higher-income households are exacerbating differences in learning opportunities *and* outcomes among children and youth. More significant, household characteristics increasingly attenuate intergenerational social mobility, long the operational definition of the "American Dream."[19] Although household education and income have not been the only factors involved, intergenerational stagnation in income brackets increased from 30 percent in the 1970s, to 37 percent in the 1980s, to 40 percent in the 1990s.[20]

Fifth, regardless of income level and geographic location, and perhaps in response to dimming prospects for intergenerational social mobility, households have been willing to physically relocate to better their life chances, including improving their work and schooling opportunities. Similar motivations are driving migration across local jurisdictions and national borders—for example, in the Southwest and from Asia, from countrysides to industrial cores, among metropolitan areas from "brawn" to "brain" cities, from urban centers to suburban rings, and from low-performing to higher-performing schools.[21] Although household choices of residence are income constrained, the pursuit of residential preferences is increasing in part because the consequences of *not* choosing have increased. Migration is not new, but the consequences of not migrating are. Where you live increasingly influences schooling and peer group quality, social capital development, and, therefore, life chances.

Changes in Government

Like households, governments see education as more consequential now than 50 years ago, and for generally similar reasons. Over the last half century government's emphasis on education has changed from sole provider to "only" primary provider and significant investor. Though public-sector enrollment as a share of total school enrollment has remained relatively stable at the margin, government bodies are increasingly accommodating the creation of alternatives to publicly provided schooling (from homeschooling to various school choice programs). Why? First, governments are now competing with each other and are thus compelled to respond, if only weakly, to household demands for improved schooling choices. Residential choice is both a cause and a consequence of intergovernmental schooling inequalities. If governments don't respond, they risk an exit from their jurisdictions of those households with the greatest desire for "improved" (or simply different) schooling options. Whether a particular government jurisdiction is, in the short run, better or worse off as a consequence of that residential "brain drain" depends largely on the makeup of its tax base and its public spending obligations. The basic point remains. Friedman's reference to governments as "the state," while technically correct then and now, masks the increasingly competitive nature of separate governmental jurisdictions. Cities, counties, regional government agencies, states, nations, and continental alliances all compete with each other to grow their tax bases and, thereby, their tax revenues. The primary means of achieving such growth is to attract "foreign" direct investment by touting the educational quality of their workforce and the quality of their educational infrastructure, among other features. The "public" nature of public goods is shaped more *within* than across jurisdictions, as governmental jurisdictions must worry first about the public within their borders, both as providers of tax revenues and as contributors to the public good within the jurisdiction. Public education goods that derive directly from *private* benefits of education (i.e., personal income that yields spending and taxable income) are of increasing concern to governments. From the perspective of government, public and private benefits of education are now more closely associated with each other. More of one generates more of the other. It's no longer so much "either/or," if it ever really was.

This is not to suggest that the public benefits associated with general citizenship are now less valued. Increased educational levels of citizens have always yielded numerous important, if not easily measured, public goods, or positive externalities, including increased propensity to vote and increased likelihood of volunteering. Rather it is to suggest that governments, like households and businesses, are compelled to compete more aggressively now than 50 years ago to achieve acceptable levels of human and social capital. Growth in both forms of capital is self-reinforcing and promotes still higher levels in the future. Increases in social and human capital also expand the tax base while reducing public costs associated with low levels of these forms of capital. Governments can increase social and human capital by "growing" them or by "attracting" them. For those reasons, and because of wage premiums associated with higher levels of schooling, governments have to provide improved educational options (among other public goods) if they are to compete successfully.

Second, in response to competitive pressures and sometimes over the objections of K–12 education officials, governments have gradually moved from a posture of *100 percent* funding and *sole* provision to one of *primary* funding and provision coupled with greater emphasis on monitoring and overseeing the performance of all education providers. Not surprisingly, the supply of publicly authorized schooling alternatives, public and private, has begun to grow. When Friedman made his voucher proposal, Edison schools weren't even imagined, homeschooling was illegal in about two-thirds of the states, magnet schools had just made their debut, charter schools were unheard of, voluntary interdistrict transfer plans were in their infancy, virtual (online) public schooling did not yet exist, and neither did voucher plans for public and private schools. Today homeschooling is a legal option in all 50 states; districts are fashioning "choice policies" for parents in their districts; and charter schools, corporately owned and managed schools, virtual schooling, and voucher plans are growing—all foreshadowing Friedman's "healthy variety" of choices.

Collectively, all of those initiatives still represent a small fraction of schools and students, and per Friedman's original proposal their growth can be seen as "gradual." His argument for gradualness was twofold. One, a "gradual and easy" transition to "denationalization" allows time for the suppliers of schooling alternatives to respond, providing competing models against which to compare publicly run schools.[22] Two, the gradual pace of transformation has provided governments time to convert their role from that of largely direct provider to the more appropriate one of efficient and effective overseer and monitor of eligible schools and administrator of voucher-related machinery. The second argument, made manifest in recent years by state level accountability plans and the No Child Left Behind Act, is also unfolding gradually, but the growth of the public oversight role in schooling is as important for voucher initiatives as is the decline of the hegemony of public school operation.

Indeed, over most of the last 50 years, poor school performance year after year was not officially monitored or sanctioned—until relatively recently, some years after the 1983 public acknowledgement of schooling problems, "A Nation at Risk." Acting as much from enlightened self-interest as for the public good, government officials have begun not only to permit, and even to foster, the creation of schooling options but to install performance and accountability systems that identify how well the (growing varieties of) schools are performing. Still far from effective, such systems cannot yet ascertain the *value added* contribution that schools make to individual student learning and are just beginning to identify and act on behalf of students who are being *systematically* underserved year after year. Governments are increasingly compelled to permit households greater choice in schooling when locally assigned public schools continue to perform poorly. For their part, households feel increasingly compelled to seek quality school choices, whether or not government provides them.

Implications of Change

What do we infer from those educational, household, and government trends as we reconsider Milton Friedman's seminal proposal for vouchers and school choice? More concretely, which details of

18

Friedman's 50-year-old proposal, if any, bear scrutiny in light of those changes? At a somewhat superficial level, a convincing argument can be made that vouchers and choice not only were a good idea at the time; they are an even better idea now. Furthermore, the idea is becoming a slow but sure reality. The basic arguments for shifting public support to the demand side from the provider side are slowly taking hold, and the manifestations of a "gradual" shift to vouchers and school choice are clear to see, if slow.

Because so much of the devil has always been in the details or parameters of specific voucher proposals, it is those parameters, rather than the basic idea, that might fall victim to any "shelf-life" problem. Indeed, at a more granular level, the trend toward vouchers over a 50-year period can mask several possibly consequential new realities, such as those outlined earlier, that could alter the value of specific voucher proposals. The trends in education and their relation to households and governments suggest consideration of at least three elements or outgrowths of the original proposal, involving, respectively, the *levels* of education for which vouchers are provided; the *variability in value*, if any, of the vouchers; and the *content* of education programs eligible for support by vouchers.

Vouchers for Which Levels of Education?

First, for well over a half century, the years of schooling deemed worthy of public support have been K–12. An argument can be made that the span of schooling deemed worthy of public support and compulsion should be expanded "downward" below full-day kindergarten and "upward" beyond 12th grade. Given what we now know about the enormous (public and private) benefits that can be derived from early childhood education (not simply child care), the concept of parental choice with public subsidy should be extended "downward" to younger children as it has been in Pennsylvania and Florida. The economic benefits are both public (e.g., reduced crime and less reliance on social services and remedial health services) and private (e.g., improved school performance in the traditional K-12 years and beyond). Because the neighborhood effects of increased schooling have grown over the years far beyond the education provided by high schools, voucher initiatives should consider support of schooling into what we now think of as the early years of college, not unlike several state and federal programs.

Vouchers Sensitive to Economic Conditions of Households?

The combined effects of increased inequality in household income, increasing household investment in education, household effects on educational achievement, and increased returns to schooling suggest consideration of means-tested vouchers. Although this issue was not directly addressed in Friedman's original article, in recent decades it has surfaced as a politically and socially significant variable in the development and implementation of voucher initiatives. The neighborhood effects argument that Friedman marshaled for the *general* voucher proposal a half century ago seems to apply, at least in part, to some form of *means-tested* or even "circumstance-tested" voucher, such as those awarded to families in some places today when their assigned schools are deemed "failing" or low performing. Growing differentials in "circumstance," plus its major impact on educational achievement, argue that some attention be paid to circumstance.

Given the role that household income plays today in differentiating education (and life) chances, addressing such disparities through means-tested vouchers may be a more educationally (if not politically) effective strategy than forcing attendance in systemically low-performing schools.

Of course, household income is highly correlated with attendance in systemically low-performing schools, and so an argument can be made on politically pragmatic grounds to use the circumstances test. This argument is not identical to Friedman's, however. The argument for a means-tested, publicly provided voucher is that universal, uniform-value vouchers can no longer provide a "level enough" playing field in schooling, given the growing disparities among households and among the public schools and districts that currently provide 90 percent of our schooling.

Vouchers for "Vocational" As Well As "General" Education?

Friedman argued in 1955 that vouchers should provide for *general* education, but not strictly *vocational* education, on the grounds that the former provided much more tangible public benefits (neighborhood effects), whereas strictly vocational education produced largely private benefits. That element of Friedman's proposal has not generated the same intensity of analysis as has his main idea. Nonetheless, along with other elements of his proposal, the *content* of education eligible for voucher support should be reconsidered. The theoretical distinction between a broad comprehensive education and a narrow vocational one can be easily made, but the automatic designation of one as providing significantly more public benefits than the other is less clear today than in the past for two reasons, one pragmatic and the other somewhat more theoretical. First, the blend of "general" and "vocational" elements in today's educational enterprises is extremely difficult to parse, except in extreme curricular and programmatic instances. That is true even at the elementary level (e.g., in the fields of reading, math, and science) and more so at the secondary level with specialty tracks ranging from highly vocational "work-study" programs to college prep, which is arguably just as vocationally oriented as the work-study programs.

The administrative machinery (and political transaction costs) necessary to distinguish between general and vocational education seems to outweigh the value of any precision that might be gained by such an effort. The issue may, however, be more fundamental than logistical. If it is the case that government provision of public goods has come to depend more on increased tax revenues from a more highly educated citizenry (read workforce), that is, on the private goods (including earnings) generated by its citizens, then citizens who took a "purely vocational" education, and who captured the resulting wage premiums, would nonetheless be significant contributors to the "public good" via greater taxes paid, fewer public services consumed, and more nominally civic behavior because of their higher economic stake in society. Although a practical distinction between public and private benefits from education is hard to make and administer, resorting to a distinction between general and vocational schooling as a proxy for them is both practically and theoretically difficult.

All three reconsiderations—level, means testing, and content—build on and derive from the original voucher proposal by Friedman. Each deals more with nontrivial but nonetheless derivative issues associated with Friedman's 1955 voucher proposal. These considerations are more salient today largely because of societal changes over time. At the risk of overplaying the shelf-life metaphor, recalibrating these three elements of Friedman's voucher proposal may add "preservatives" to it that will prolong its already long shelf life. Indeed, these and other amplifications of the school voucher idea might even have the effect of getting more versions of it off the shelf and into the classroom.

Notes

1. See, for example, William G. Howell and Paul E. Peterson, *The Education Gap: Vouchers and Urban Schools* (Washington: Brookings Institution Press, 2002); C. M. Hoxby, *The Economics of School Choice* (Chicago: University of Chicago Press, 2003); H. Levin, *Privatizing Education: Can the Marketplace Deliver Freedom of Choice, Efficiency, Equity, and Social Cohesion?* (Boulder, CO: Westview, 2001); and E. G. West, "Education Vouchers in Practice and Principle: A World Survey," World Bank Human Capital Development and Operations Policy Working Papers, February 1996, http://worldbank.org/html/extdr/hnp/hddflash/workp/wp_00064.html.

2. Milton Friedman, "The Role of Government in Education," in *Economics and the Public Interest*, ed. Robert A. Solo (New Brunswick, NJ: Rutgers University Press, 1955), p. 124.

3. Ibid.

4. Ibid., p. 127.

5. Ibid., p. 130.

6. Ibid., p. 129.

7. Patrick J. McEwan, "The Potential Impact of Vouchers," *Peabody Journal of Education* 79, no. 3 (2004): 57–80.

8. Jennifer Cheesman Day and Eric C. Newburger, *The Big Payoff: Educational Attainment and Synthetic Estimates of Work-Life Earnings* (Washington: U.S. Bureau of the Census, 2002).

9. Gary Becker, "Human Capital and Poverty," *Religion and Liberty* 8, no. 1 (1998): 1–7.

10. Lynn A. Karoly and Constantijn W. A. Panis, *The 21st Century at Work: Forces Shaping the Future Workforce and Workplace in the United States* (Santa Monica, CA: RAND Corporation, 2004).

11. Kati Haycock, "Ticket to Nowhere: The Gap between Leaving High School and Entering College and High-Performance Jobs," *Thinking K–16* (Education Trust) 3, no. 2 (Fall 1999), http://www2.edtrust.org/EdTrust/Press + Room/high + school.htm.

12. Robert Lynch, *Exceptional Returns: Economic, Fiscal, and Social Benefits of Investment in Early Childhood Development* (Washington: Economic Policy Institute, 2004).

13. Ibid., p. vii.

14. Michael Sandler, "The Emerging Education Industry," in *Handbook of Educational Leadership and Management*, ed. Brent Davies and John West-Burnham (London: Pearson Education, 2003), chap. 28.

15. James P. Comer, "Home-School Relationships As They Affect the Academic Success of Children," *Education and Urban Society* 16, no. 3 (1984): 322–37.

16. Center for Educational Research and Innovation, *The Well-being of Nations: The Role of Human and Social Capital* (Paris: Organization for Economic Cooperation and Development, 2001).

17. Paul Krugman, "The Death of Horatio Alger," *Nation*, January 5, 2004, http://www.thenation.com/docprint.mhtml?i = 20040105&s = krugman; and Kerwin K. Charles and Erik Hurst, "The Correlation of Wealth across Generations," *Journal of Political Economy* 111, no. 6 (2003): 1155–82.

18. David Wessel, "As Rich-Poor Gap Widens in the U.S., Class Mobility Stalls," *Wall Street Journal*, May 13, 2005, pp. A1, A7.

19. Ibid.

20. Aaron Bernstein, "Waking Up from the American Dream: Meritocracy and Equal Opportunity Are Fading Fast," *Business Week,* December 1, 2003, http://reclaimdemocracy.org/weekly_2003/american_dream_death.html.

21. Center for Educational Research and Innovation, *Cities and Regions in the New Learning Economy* (Paris: Organization for Economic Cooperation and Development, 2001); Milken Institute, *8th Annual Global Conference: Briefing Book* (Santa Monica, CA: Milken Institute, 2005); Allan Williams et al., "International Labor Mobility and Uneven Regional Development in Europe: Human Capital, Knowledge and Entrepreneurship," *European Urban and Regional Studies* 11, no. 1 (2004): 27–46; and M. Kritz and F. Caces, "Science and Technology Transfers and Migration Flows," in *International Migration Systems: A Global Approach,* ed. Kritz, Lim, and Zlotnik (Oxford: Clarendon, 1992), pp. 221–44.

22. Friedman, p. 132.

2. Choice, Religion, Community, and Educational Quality

John E. Brandl

In his remarkable essay of 50 years ago, Milton Friedman foresaw much of the subsequent debate over choice in education. However, in our time, the arguments that will determine whether choice will become widespread policy may be somewhat different from those employed by Friedman in 1955. His stance at the time was both individualistic ("I shall assume a society that takes freedom of the individual . . . as its ultimate objective") and theoretical (there was no recourse to empirical research in the essay). In this essay, I will first take note of Friedman's prescience. I will then offer explanations for why choice is not more widely permitted. Finally, I will suggest that, if a policy of school choice catches on in America any time soon, it may be because a form of communitarian argument provides a complementary but politically more persuasive case than the line of reasoning originally used by Friedman. In doing this I will draw on contemporary empirical evidence regarding the efficacy of choice.

Many of Friedman's insights were novel in 1955 and remain powerful and influential today. Consider his simple observation that when the private sector does not spontaneously undertake to produce a publicly valuable service, and government action is required, the government need not be both funder and producer of the service.[1] Having a governmental entity as funder alone and leaving production to a different, perhaps private, body opens the way to contracting for results rather than resorting to bureaucratic production. Contrast that with the conflict of interest embodied in the typical arrangement in American public education. School boards have the responsibility to see to it that children receive quality instruction, but instead of contracting with the best available producers of educational services, they generally buy almost exclusively from themselves. The services they purchase are produced in schools they own and operate.

Addressing that inherent conflict of interest by creating a funder-producer split lies at the heart of one of contemporary America's most promising educational reforms, charter schools. In 1955 Friedman not only argued the necessity of a funder-producer split but also anticipated the possibility that in some instances both halves of the split would be governmental.[2] The appropriateness of a funder-producer split was very much on the minds of the inventors of charter schools.[3]

In 1990 there were no charter schools in the country. Today there are more than 3,600.[4] A charter school is not private; rather, it is a form of governmental entity with which a local school board or state government or other organization empowered by state law contracts to produce education. If the agreed-upon educational results are not achieved in the period of time stipulated in the contract or charter, the organization with which the charter school had contracted is free to go elsewhere for the desired service.

A policy of charter schools is different from but complementary to a policy of student choice among public schools. Friedman's essay also presaged the latter development, 30 years before the first legislation permitting statewide public school choice was passed (in Minnesota) in 1985.[5]

Although they expand schooling options, charter schools and public school choice ultimately fall short of Friedman's ideal case, individual choice for elementary and secondary students from among both public and private schools, with government funds following the students. Friedman has hardly kept secret his conviction that market choice fosters efficiency, but in his 1955 essay his chief rationale for choice was not instrumental but simply that freedom is good in itself.

Evidently, that argument has not been powerful enough to sway American policymakers even though some polls find that a majority of Americans favor school choice.[6] That majority is not organized into an interest group, a severe handicap in changing policy when lobbyists for the country's millions of public school employees understandably and strenuously resist legislation that would strengthen their competitors. When I was a state legislator in Minnesota, no other interest group was as successful in advancing its cause. The power of the public school lobby is but one reason why neither major U.S. political party has made school choice a central objective.

Delving further into this matter will help us understand the education problem in America.

These days there is an abundance of maps of the United States on which the political leanings of regions are represented. They show large central cities, Democratic strongholds, in blue and most of the rest of the country, Republican, in red. Those delineations roughly depict the educational achievement gap as well. The poor, at any rate those of color, are concentrated in cities, and sadly they achieve at levels much lower than do more affluent whites (and some Asians). The achievement gap between whites on the one hand and blacks and Hispanics on the other narrowed in the 1970s and 1980s but by some measures has widened since then.[7] The Education Commission of the States summarizes: "By the end of high school, black and Hispanic students' reading and mathematics skills are roughly the same as those of white students in 8th grade."[8] That is the great problem of American education, and neither Republicans nor Democrats have effectively addressed it.

For decades Republicans more than Democrats have endorsed market solutions to social problems, so it might be expected that they would actively advance school choice as the most promising educational reform. Perhaps because low educational achievement occurs disproportionately in "blue America," few Republican politicians appear to feel a need to take on the issue. Instead, their approach to educational choice rests in the operation of a market of another kind—that in real estate. Local property taxes form a large portion of school funding across America, with revenues tied to schools in each local district. Surrounding the typical American metropolis are suburbs, populated by people with the means to afford large, comfortable homes and outfitted with attractive schools funded in part from property taxes on those highly valued homes. Politicians serving those areas—typically in "red America"—do not have to champion school choice; their constituents already have the homes, and evidently think they have the schools, they want.

The more interesting question is why Democrats solidly oppose educational choice. After all, they cannot fail to see the calamitous condition of education in the central cities. Some Democrats have proposed that public school choice might redress this inequity, but even where state law permits students to attend public school outside their home districts—which is not yet common—few inner-city

27

families are attracted by the prospect of transferring their children to what appears to be an inhospitable or alien school miles away in suburbia. In fact, inner-city African Americans, a group whom Democrats purport to champion, support a Friedman-style form of choice by a wide margin.[9] But impoverished African Americans are no more organized as an interest group than are others with whom they agree on this issue. Meanwhile, African-American leaders, perhaps because many hold important positions within the public school system, oppose choice[10] and largely support the Democratic Party, as do public school teachers' unions. The latter are so well organized that it is rare for a Democrat to defy them. Terry Moe has advanced the conjecture that eventually the Democratic Party will rethink whether to support the position of ordinary African Americans or that of the teachers' unions on this issue. He predicts that, when the former express their position more strenuously, the party will side with them, the larger group, and finally the country will get school choice.[11]

In the meantime, we may posit and try to understand the existence of another important underlying reason for the resistance of the Democratic Party to vouchers: the continuing influence of John Dewey.

If in the past century Milton Friedman has been the most influential proponent of the good to be accomplished through the use of markets in America. John Dewey was his earlier counterpart in giving encouragement to those who would accomplish good not through markets but through government. In the early decades of the 20th century Dewey foresaw the coming expansion of government and supplied its workers and devotees with the optimism of the title of his 1934 book, *A Common Faith*.[12] For Dewey, science had shown the claims to truth of traditional religion—Christianity in particular, but he also mentions Judaism and Islam by name—to be nonsense.[13] Progress meant "emancipation" from all "encumbrances" having anything to do with the supernatural.[14] Other features of religion, however, especially its ability to stimulate effort and altruism, remained so valuable that "religious" became one of Dewey's favorite words. He used the term "God" to denote "the unity of all ideal ends arousing us to desire and action."[15] Armed with secular enthusiasm and unburdened of the obscurantist religious doctrines of the past, Americans could overcome whatever social maladies beset the country. Government's bureaus would be the agents of a decent people. The public schools would be the shrines in which all would be encouraged, supported, and fulfilled.

Many people in government today—whether or not affiliated with conventional religion—appear still to be imbued with Dewey's "devotion . . . so intense as to be religious."[16] They extol and practice cooperation. They justify their lives through service. For them, government's bureaus do manifest a generous country's good will.

And yet, somewhere John Dewey is rubbing his eyes in astonishment, for not only do the major faiths continue to hold the allegiance of millions, but in some cases they carry out public functions better than does government. That is not easy for devotees of the common faith to accept. They had expected the demise of the inspirational force of traditional religions, which, in turn, would be succeeded by a national secular religion with governmental institutions, especially the schools, as its temples.

As it turns out, another aspect of Dewey's thought could be helpful here in pointing a way forward: he was less interested in truth, religious or otherwise, than in determining what works.[17] Try things. See what happens. Test. Measure. Go with whatever succeeds. Dewey is representative of American pragmatism, which calls for what actually works to take precedence when we judge the appropriateness of a policy.

So, what *does* work in education, Dewey's ideal of national purpose realized through government's bureaus or Friedman's ideal of freedom realized through market choice? It is difficult to make a case for today's educational bureaus, comprised of public schools, usually monopolies, funded not directly by the recipients of their services but by legislatures and school boards. After adjusting for inflation, the amount of money devoted to today's average student is double what was allotted to the schooling of that child's parents 35 years ago.[18] So much more is being spent now, and so slight has been the change in academic achievement, that for much of the last quarter century perhaps the dominant impression among careful researchers was that in elementary and secondary education no statistical relationship exists between spending and results.[19]

In recent years, a more nuanced and somewhat more encouraging understanding of the situation has emerged. Larry V. Hedges and Rob Greenwald have made a counterargument that has come to be accepted by many who evaluate the effectiveness of the schools: more money, spent carefully, can and does have a positive effect.[20] For example, the Effective Schools Movement of the 1970s and 1980s set out to identify a number of characteristics of more successful schools and found that those characteristics included strong leadership, an orderly environment, the teaching of basic skills, high expectations of students, homework regularly assigned and completed, a substantial part of the students' day spent on academic work, systematic monitoring of students' progress, and a sense on the part of students, teachers, and parents that their school is a community.[21]

Unfortunately, although the efficacy of those practices is now well-known, they do not characterize our schools; much expenditure on schooling goes to items unproven to correlate with better education for children. This is the Achilles' heel of the public schools. They do not systematically make use of approaches known to be effective. Some perform well, but in general they lack a mechanism, a lever, that would stimulate innovation and efficiency. Dewey's common faith, long considered the bedrock support for public education, has not been strong enough to keep the public schools from sliding. Perhaps employing his pragmatism will prove more successful, but it requires giving school choice a fair test.

Proponents of markets argue that the competition inherent in school choice provides just such a device for fostering innovation and efficiency. Caroline Hoxby has conducted the most sophisticated studies of public school choice. An economist, she expects competition to improve efficiency, and that is indeed what she finds in schools. Comparing U.S. metropolitan areas and statistically adjusting for differences in income, race, and other potentially confounding variables, she finds student test scores higher in those areas that permit the most choice than in those that do not permit any. Interestingly, she calculates that, on average, the competitive, higher-performing districts spend less per child.[22]

Not everyone is convinced. Hoxby's most spirited critic, the equally distinguished economist Helen Ladd, believes that turning education over to the market is potentially damaging to children. Ladd makes two arguments: (1) Since education is compulsory, and successful schools do not have the incentives to expand that successful firms have, those students left behind in poor schools would do worse when their luckier peers got into better schools. (2) Many parents would want to move their children to schools in which the socioeconomic status of the families is higher than in their current schools. That would result in a "hierarchy of schools" that, again, would be detrimental to those left behind.[23] Hoxby's rejoinder is twofold: (1) The current educational system has long since effectively abandoned the most disadvantaged children, trapping them in schools that are not enabling them to catch up with their privileged contemporaries. (2) In any event, says Hoxby, her evidence shows competition is so powerful that it particularly benefits those schools from which some children move. She gives examples of cities where disadvantaged children who stayed in schools newly subject to competition achieved at higher levels than previously.

With the argument coming to turn around the challenge of educating the most disadvantaged, we should consider what else we know about how the academic achievement of such youngsters might be improved. Forty years ago James Coleman showed that family characteristics are far stronger influences on the educational lives of children than is school.[24] The vast increases in appropriations for education over the subsequent four decades reflect a continuing reluctance to confront that fact. Meanwhile, throughout that period, there have been indications here and there that in sectarian schools many disadvantaged students do well.[25] Objections to this are raised by those still partaking of Dewey's common faith. For example, if youngsters perform better in religious schools, surely it is only because they are the more easily educated students, creamed off from the public schools, and even if they receive an educational boost, they have missed out on the development of tolerance and civic virtue that takes place in public education's melting pot. Besides, argue some defenders of public education, when children leave public schools—particularly if funding leaves with them—those who remain are harmed.

One by one, those concerns are being turned into research questions and settled by evidence. Religious schools appear to be particularly successful with some disadvantaged African Americans even where random assignment eliminates the creaming concern.[26] On average, private schools, almost all of which are religious, are more racially integrated than are public schools. Children attending private schools are more apt to tolerate anti-religious activities, more willing to favor members of their least-liked group being permitted to participate in public affairs, more inclined to speak and write on public issues, and more involved in volunteer work. On average, they are at least as well prepared as their public school counterparts for productive life in a diverse society.[27]

All that is accomplished at about half the cost—not tuition but full cost—of the public schools, even without counting special education, transportation, and much of central administration, all big financial burdens for public education.[28] Consequently, granting poor children government funds for use at religious schools could actually *improve* the fiscal condition of public education. Each child who left the public schools would take along to a religious school many thousands of dollars less than the current funding per student. Thus, average funds available for students in public schools could rise. That could be politically attractive in the era the country is now entering. The demographics of the coming decades, when a smaller fraction of the population in the workforce will support a larger fraction of the old and young, will make reducing the cost of public services even more appealing to the citizenry than it was in times when the workforce was growing rapidly.

So the evidence shows that some children, particularly among the disadvantaged, do better in sectarian schools. Since spending in those schools is so low, even if children's achievement there were merely equal to that of their peers in public school, the cost-effectiveness of sectarian schools would be far superior to that of any other educational reform including public school choice.

Friedman failed to anticipate this development, predicting in 1955 that because sectarian schools were about a different purpose than education, eventually "private enterprise" would "be far more efficient. . . . The final result may therefore well be less rather than more parochial education."[29] Neither he nor Dewey foresaw the continuing ability of organized religion to educate children both in academic basics and for democratic citizenship.

How can sectarian schools do it? Evidently something besides competition is at work. Perhaps sectarian schools are communities generating and dispensing inspiration and nurture that accomplishes much that money cannot buy.[30]

Perhaps sectarian schools provide some disadvantaged children with a substitute for the care they are not receiving from family and neighborhood—something possible but very rare in public schools.

Yes, many children are thriving in public school, but a disproportionate number of disadvantaged children are not. Education in a sectarian school, the very practice Dewey and others sought to make impossible through public education, would be a step up for some of those now falling behind in public school, trapped there because they are incapable of paying private school tuition.

Perhaps, then, the inspiration of community, not the discipline of competition, is the central explanation for the efficacy of choice. Like freedom, community has worth in itself but can also be instrumentally useful. Fortunately, sometimes freedom and community are complementary and we are not compelled to choose between them. Educational choice is one such instance. Freedom of choice enables families to find the community in which their children can thrive. Few principled objections remain to giving poor children the choice the affluent already have to attend the school that fits them best. Friedman's proposal of 50 years ago remains the most promising education reform for America.

Notes

The author thanks J. T. Haines, his coauthor on an earlier study of education policy.

1. Milton Friedman, "The Role of Government in Education," in *Economics and the Public Interest,* ed. Robert A. Solo (New Brunswick, NJ: Rutgers University Press, 1955), p. 127.

2. Ibid., pp. 128–30.

3. See Ted Kolderie, *Creating the Capacity for Change: How and Why Governors and Legislatures Are Opening a New-Schools Sector in Public Education* (Bethesda, MD: Education Week Press, 2005).

4. Center for Education Reform, "Making Schools Work Better for All Children: Charter Schools," 2006, http://edreform.com/index.cfm?fuseAction = stateStats& pSectionID = Is&cSectionID = 44.

5. Friedman proposed as well that higher education be funded not by appropriations to institutions but by aiding individual students, though that was less novel since it followed by several years the enactment of the GI Bill for veterans returning from World War II. Friedman suggested a way that students could later be required to repay the support thus received. Each aided student could "pay to the government in each future year x percent of his earnings in excess of y dollars for each $1000 that he gets in this way." Friedman also hinted at a drawback that could cause such a repayment scheme to founder: students intending to go into low-paying professions would gladly sign up for the aid while those who expected high future earnings would look elsewhere for funding. Friedman, pp. 140–41.

6. See Terry M. Moe, *Schools, Vouchers and the American Public* (Washington: Brookings Institution Press, 2001), chap. 7.

7. U.S. Department of Education, National Center of Educational Statistics, *National Assessment of Educational Progress, 2001,* Summary Data Tables.

8. Education Commission of the States, "Closing the Achievement Gap," 2005.

9. Moe, pp. 214–15.

10. Ibid., pp. 383–84.

11. Ibid., pp. 383–88.

12. John Dewey, *A Common Faith* (New Haven, CT: Yale University Press, 1934).

13. Ibid., pp. 4, 8.

14. Ibid., pp. 8–9.

15. Ibid., p. 42.

16. Ibid., p. 79.

17. See John Dewey, "Valuation and Experimental Knowledge," in *John Dewey: The Middle Works, 1899–1924*, ed. Jo Ann Boydston (Carbondale and Edwardsville: Southern Illinois University Press, 1983), vol. 13, 1921–1922.

18. Hanna Skandera and Richard Sousa, *School Figures: The Data behind the Debate* (Stanford, CA: Hoover Institution Press, 2003), p. 198.

19. See Eric A. Hanushek, "The Economics of Schooling: Production and Efficiency in Public Schools," *Journal of Economic Literature* 24 (1986): 1141–47; and *Does Money Matter? The Effect of School Resources on Student Achievement and Adult Success*, ed. Gary Burtless (Washington: Brookings Institution Press, 1996).

20. See Larry V. Hedges and Rob Greenwald, "Have Times Changed?" in *Does Money Matter?*

21. John Brandl, *Money and Good Intentions Are Not Enough: Or Why a Liberal Democrat Thinks States Need Both Competition and Community* (Washington: Brookings Institution Press, 1998), p. 32 and references there.

22. See Caroline Hoxby, "Rising Tide," *Education Next*, 2001, www.educationnext.org/20014068.html; and "School Choice and School Competition: Evidence from the United States," *Swedish Economic Policy Review*, 2002, pp. 10, 11–67.

23. Helen Ladd, "Comment on Caroline Hoxby, 'School Choice and School Competition: Evidence from the United States,'" *Swedish Economic Policy Review*, 2002, pp. 11, 67–76.

24. See James Coleman et al., *Equality of Educational Opportunity* (Washington: U.S. Department of Health, Education and Welfare, 1966).

25. Brandl, p. 107 and references there.

26. William G. Howell and Paul E. Peterson, *The Education Gap: Vouchers and Urban Schools* (Washington: Brookings Institution Press, 2002); see especially chap. 6.

27. See Jay Greene, "The Surprising Consensus on School Choice," *Public Interest* 144 (2001): 19–35; and Jay Greene, "Civic Values in Public and Private Schools," in *Learning from School Choice*, ed. Paul E. Peterson and Bryan C. Hassel (Washington: Brookings Institution Press, 1998).

28. Michael Garet et al., "The Determinants of Per-Pupil Expenditures in Private Elementary and Secondary Schools: An Exploratory Analysis," National Center for Education Statistics Working Paper 97-07, March, 1997; U.S. Department of Education, National Center for Educational Statistics, *National Assessment of Educational Progress, 1997*, Table 3; and Howell and Peterson, pp. 91–99.

29. Friedman, p. 129.

30. See James Coleman and Thomas Hoffer, *Public and Private High Schools: The Impact of Communities* (New York: Basic Books, 1987); Paul T. Hill, Gail E. Foster, and Tamar Gendler, *High Schools with Character*, RAND Report R-3944-RC (Santa Monica, CA: RAND Corporation, 1990); and Anthony S. Bryk, Valerie E. Lee, and Peter B. Holland, *Catholic Schools and the Common Good* (Cambridge, MA: Harvard University Press, 1993).

3. A Culture of Choice

Abigail Thernstrom

How do we decide who is middle class in America? Here's a simple test: Do the children attend schools their parents have chosen? Does the family have enough money to select a place of residence with acceptable schools or, alternatively, to pay private or parochial school tuition?

Only low-income parents have little or no say in the education their kids receive. Only they are stuck with schools that no child should be forced to attend. Moreover, the children who pay the heaviest price for that lack of choice are those who come to school with the least—namely, urban black and Latino youngsters. It is precisely those underprivileged children who most need the privilege of school choice.

Advocates of school choice make a number of arguments—the inextricable link between choice and freedom, the benefits of competition, the value of letting numerous educational flowers bloom. I buy all of them. But I would add another: Choice is the precondition for the growth of a particular brand of school that seems to work best for the at-risk black and Latino kids who are alarmingly behind their white and Asian peers throughout their academic careers. It's a brand of schooling that seems most effective not only at instilling academic skills and knowledge but also at promoting "the common set of values" that Milton Friedman, 50 years ago, saw as essential to the survival of "a stable and democratic society."

The freedom of individuals to make choices, with the understanding that choices have consequences, is central to the American creed, but that creed is only weakly understood by the typical inner-city black student. The task of connecting ghetto kids with the basic American belief in choice and responsibility is arguably made harder when the government has placed grave limits on their educational options. How can they be schooled in the importance of individual freedom when they have been conscripted into the public institution that governs much of their day?

Black and Hispanic students, whether their families are affluent or low income, are typically far behind whites and Asians, and part of the problem is their disconnect from mainstream American values. In a nation in which the doors of opportunity are so remarkably open, we still have a racially identifiable group of educational have-nots, children whose life prospects will inevitably be stunted by their inadequate schooling in both skills and values. It used to be thought that social class divided the educationally successful from those who tended to founder in school. Hence the high hopes attached to anti-poverty programs such as Title I. But after taking full account of racial differences in poverty rates, parental education, and place of residence, something like two-thirds of the troubling racial gap remains unexplained. Much of that unexplained gap, I argue below, is the result of a culture that leaves black kids deeply alienated from the values and habits that make for academic success.

This essay focuses on inner-city African Americans because, typically, their prospects for academic success seem the bleakest. Hispanics are immigrants and over time they seem to be moving up the economic ladder, in much the same fashion as Italians and other newcomers with limited education and educational aspirations did in the past. But there are no grounds for complacency about the future of descendants of American slaves, whose difficulties in school seem more deeply rooted and harder to remedy than those of any other group. Moreover, the future of black children is, rightly, a matter of moral as well as economic concern—given America's long history of racial oppression.

Either these children will catch up with their academically more successful peers, or ancient inequalities will continue to corrupt the fabric of American society and undermine its democratic functioning and stability. Although cures for the problem litter the educational landscape, in fact, most are close to useless for a simple reason: they amount to tinkering with the current system—taking the current structure of public education as a given and trying to improve it. Conventional solutions will not do. Rather, a package of radical educational reforms is needed, with school choice as an indispensable element.

36

Racial Gap in Academic Achievement

Not long ago, the racial gap in academic achievement was a hush-hush topic—visible, in fact, only to a few academics. The civil rights organizations, if they knew the picture, were certainly not talking about it—perhaps out of fear that the data would be viewed through a racist lens. Problems not addressed are not solved, however, and the issue quite suddenly, in one of those mysterious historical turning points, has acquired top billing on the nation's educational agenda.

Closing the gap is thus the core purpose of the No Child Left Behind Act, the 2001 revision of the omnibus 1965 Elementary and Secondary Education Act. It's true that the preamble refers to other achievement gaps as well—for instance, that which separates affluent and low-income kids. But the central issue, everyone knows, is the yawning gap in skills and knowledge between whites and Asians, on the one hand, and blacks and Hispanics, on the other hand.

The best evidence on the magnitude of the gap comes from the National Assessment of Educational Progress, often called "the nation's report card." Created by Congress in 1969, NAEP regularly tests nationally representative samples of American elementary and secondary school students in the 4th, 8th, and 12th grades (or sometimes at ages 9, 13, and 17). In considering the data—some of which are provided below—it is important to remember two obvious points. In every group some students are academically talented, while others founder; nevertheless, group averages—whether the subject is education or poverty—are important. But group averages are not the product of fixed, innate traits that are independent of the environment and cannot be changed. The racial gap in academic achievement is a problem that can be solved; there is a way, if we have the will.

The NAEP data, available since the early 1970s, have consistently drawn an appalling picture of black and Hispanic youngsters left behind. For instance:

- At age 17, the typical black or Hispanic student is scoring less well than at least 80 percent of his or her white classmates. On average, these non-Asian minority students are four years behind those who are white or Asian. They are finishing high school with a junior high education. Thus, the employer hiring the typical black or Latino high school graduate (or the college that admits the average non-Asian minority student) is, in effect, choosing a youngster who has made it only through eighth grade.

- In five of the seven subjects tested by NAEP, a *majority* of black students perform in the lowest category—Below Basic. That means that a majority of black students do not have even a "partial" mastery of the "fundamental" knowledge and skills expected of students in the 12th grade. Hispanic students at the end of high school do somewhat better than their black classmates, but they, too, are far behind their white and Asian peers.
- The news is no happier when we switch our gaze from students at the bottom to those at the top. Take math. In math, only 0.2 percent of black students fall into NAEP's Advanced category; the figure is 11 times higher for whites and 37 times higher for Asians. Again, Hispanic students are only a shade ahead of blacks in the proportion of high performers in every subject.

With so few blacks and Hispanics with superior academic skills by the end of high school, the pool of those ready to do the work demanded in highly selective colleges and likely to become part of the American professional and business elite is inevitably very small.

There are some more recent NAEP results suggesting improvements in learning for grades four and eight, but the scantier data available for students at the end of high school suggest that the gains have not carried over to that age. In 2004 the black-white gap in math was just one point smaller than it had been 20 years before; in reading, the 2004 gap was as wide as it had been in 1990, and 9 points greater than it had been in 1998.

Why the persistent gap, which has not narrowed since the late 1980s? Not surprisingly, different scholars give different answers. Richard Rothstein of the Economic Policy Institute is arguably today's leading spokesman for the view that most of the gap is "attributable to the fact that black families, on average, have lower social class characteristics than white families." Indeed, Rothstein argues that "the gap in average achievement can probably not be narrowed substantially as long as the United States maintains such vast differences in socioeconomic conditions." Fixing education requires eliminating the "disparities in income, health and housing"; if we fail to do so, "there is little prospect of equalizing [academic] achievement."[1]

The problem with Rothstein's view is that (as indicated earlier) several careful studies have shown that controlling for socioeconomic status reduces the gap by no more than one-third.[2] In any case, if he's right, we might as well abandon the quest for radically improved education. He wants, for starters, something done "about the wide income gap between lower- and middle-class parents," as well as "a plan to stabilize the housing of working families with children."[3] Lofty aims to be met with policies that can only be described as either pathetically piddling or politically DOA—leaving aside the question of the cost and whether they would achieve their ends.

Other explanations for the persistent racial gap in achievement include differences in school funding, class size, uncertified teachers, and the like. None of them stands up to close scrutiny.[4] But what about racial isolation, which Rothstein names as an important factor? The question is worth exploring because the widely imposed remedy for that "segregation" has been less choice, not more. Busing was an important educational policy that affected school districts across the nation starting in the late 1960s. Today, that denial of school choice in the interest of racial equity still has strong supporters within the community of advocates of civil rights and equal education, as well as elite opinion makers.

Desegregation

The desegregation story starts, of course, with *Brown v. Board of Education*. On May 17, 1954, a unanimous Supreme Court found that de jure segregation generated "a feeling of inferiority" on the part of black children that "affects their hearts and minds in a way unlikely ever to be undone." But the decision did not suggest that racial imbalance, per se, crippled their education. In fact, at its heart was an insistence that black families have more choice—the choice to go to a neighborhood school that whites attended, for instance. De jure segregation was all about restricting choice—and *Brown* about expanding it.

Nevertheless, 14 years after the decision, the desegregation of schools in the Deep South had barely begun, and the Supreme Court (in the context of the assassination of Dr. Martin Luther King Jr. and a massive wave of race riots) finally ran out of patience. The result was what Milton Friedman called "forced nonsegregation." In the North, as well as the South, judges instituted policies that denied even the minimum freedom of parents who wanted to stay in a particular city to select a school through their choice of residential neighborhood.

Thus, thousands of children, both black and white, found themselves assigned by federal courts to schools neither they nor their families had chosen.[5] The right of black parents to be free from racism in the context of educational opportunity came to justify assignment policies imposed top-down with little or no parental or even local political input. That happened in Boston, Denver, Little Rock, Norfolk, and elsewhere—everywhere courts found (or threatened to find) the intentional separation of students on the basis of race. Black and white parents became pawns in a social experiment that stripped them of all control over their kids' education.[6] "I want my freedom back," said one Boston parent after court-ordered busing began there. "They took my freedom. They tell me where my kids have to go to school. This is like living in Russia. Next they'll tell you where to shop."[7]

The drive for racial balance has lost steam but has not been abandoned. In numerous districts where parental choice is most needed, school assignments continue to be governed by concerns about "segregation." Moreover, a small scholarly industry, whose most visible author is Harvard education professor Gary Orfield, continues to generate widely reported papers arguing that, since the early 1990s, black students have become increasingly "resegregated"; "segregated schools are still highly unequal"; in big cities particularly, they "have stunningly high levels of high school dropouts and very poor records of preparing students for higher education."[8] In fact, schools are not becoming "resegregated" at all; they were, in many instances, already racially unbalanced. Moreover, given existing residential patterns, there is little chance that schools could avoid this problem and become racially balanced. Most important—putting aside the social benefits of integration—what matters in a school is not the racial mix but the academic culture and the quality of the teachers, which are not likely to change within the existing system of public education.[9]

Culturally Disadvantaged Students

Today, many advocates of desegregation do not even bother to argue that busing plans—race-based school assignments imposed by public authorities—have academic benefits for black inner-city children.[10] For good reason. Almost no evidence suggests that racial isolation explains the gap in academic achievement or that race-based school assignments—imposed by public authorities—have improved the quality of schooling for black inner-city students, who typically have distinctive educational needs that are extremely hard to meet.

Inner-city children arrive in school culturally as well as academically disadvantaged. It's a point that almost everyone knows but few people have been willing to discuss. When it comes to academic performance, members of some racial and ethnic groups are more culturally advantaged than others. Thus, in part, group cultures explain differences in academic achievement, and that explanation strengthens the case for school choice.

"Culture," it is important to stress, does not imply a fixed set of group traits. It is a loose and slippery term, easily misunderstood. I use the term to suggest values, attitudes, and skills that are shaped and reshaped by environment—an environment that includes schools. Culture matters, but it is fluid—open to change.

A 1997 National Task Force on Minority High Achievement convened by the College Board concluded that "East Asian American high school and college students . . . spend much more time on their studies outside of school and are more likely to be part of academically oriented peer groups." In addition, their "parents are more likely than Whites to train their children to believe success is based on effort rather than innate ability," and thus they instill in their children the values of hard work, "diligence, thoroughness, and self-discipline."[11] Asian children are expected to work extraordinarily hard in school, and do so, cutting classes less often than their peers, enrolling in advanced placement courses at triple the white rate, and spending twice as much time on homework as their non-Asian classmates.[12] They are the Benjamin Franklins of our time—the group that has most intensely embraced the traditional work

41

ethic. As a result, on some math tests, the white-Asian gap is actually larger than the black-white gap.

Black children typically enter kindergarten not only academically behind but less ready to conform to behavioral demands as well. The problems persist throughout their school careers. A wealth of evidence supports a picture of disproportionate numbers of abusive, disruptive African-American students, an extraordinary number of hours spent watching television, and a general disconnection from school as an avenue of social mobility.

In a speech in Chicago in 1963, the Reverend Martin Luther King Jr. offered his advice to African-American students. "When you are behind in a footrace," he said, "the only way to get ahead is to run faster than the man in front of you. So when your white roommate says he's tired and goes to sleep, you stay up and burn the midnight oil."[13]

Good advice—but largely unheeded. Black students today do not typically burn the midnight oil and run faster to catch up. Two provocative essays by Pedro Noguera of the Harvard Graduate School of Education discuss the need to "counter and transform" African-American "cultural patterns" that inhibit achievement. "A rigid connection between racial identity and school performance . . . exists in the minds of some students of color," Noguera writes. "If students regard Blackness as being equated with playing basketball and listening to rap music but not with studying geometry and chemistry, then it is unlikely that changing the school alone will do much to change achievement outcomes for students."[14] Noguera's argument, as refreshing as it is, misses an important point. He assumes that school change, which he labels as insufficient, refers to such reforms as standards and testing, altering teacher licensure provisions, and the like. But, as I will argue below, education can be altered in ways that break the connection between blackness and basketball. Schools can do more than teach the three Rs; they can "counter and transform . . . cultural patterns." But only if they are schools of choice.

Schools That Work

The nation has placed closing the achievement gap at the top of its educational agenda. However, the grab bag of conventional strategies most states have contemplated or embraced (after-school programs, summer school for kids needing remediation, professional development for teachers, and the like) is not likely to have any significant impact. Or at least no evidence so far suggests that it will. The needs of the minority children who enter kindergarten already behind run too deep to respond to limited and scattershot policies—or to the traditional focus on academic skills and knowledge alone.

Just how difficult it is to meet the needs of kids who start school academically and behaviorally unprepared is also apparent in the failure of such well-meaning programs as I Have a Dream, which promises college tuition to inner-city students who finish high school. Such programs assume that philanthropists can add some bells and whistles to the existing public school system and the children will learn. Nothing could be further from the truth.

The picture is far from entirely bleak, however. Across the country, there are excellent schools that are getting impressive results with precisely those children who are most disconnected from the world of academic learning. Those schools all look more or less alike. And all are (of necessity) schools of choice—although some are charter schools and thus technically within the public system.

The formula for such educational success is nothing but common sense. Excellent schools for inner-city students have greatly extended instructional time with more hours in the day, longer weeks, and longer years. They have terrific principals who have the authority and autonomy to manage their budgets, set salaries, staff the schools with fabulous teachers, and get rid of those who don't work out. Those schools focus relentlessly on the core academic subjects, insisting that their students learn the times tables, basic historical facts, spelling, punctuation, the rules of grammar, and the meaning of often unfamiliar words. They provide safe, orderly environments in which to teach and learn. But they also aim to shape the culture of their students, *as that culture affects academic achievement.*

They address Noguera's concern, which is shared by Harvard sociologist Orlando Patterson, among others. "The greatest problem now facing African Americans is their isolation from the tacit norms of the dominant culture," Patterson has written.[15] Education as a means of connecting African-American children to the dominant culture is not a new idea, Thomas Sowell points out in his recent book *Black Rednecks and White Liberals*. Teachers from religious missionary associations in New England poured into the South immediately after the end of the Civil War. Their avowed purpose was cultural transformation—teaching "the Yankee virtues of industry and thrift," as well as correct English, a courteous demeanor, and refined manners.[16]

Superior schools in today's inner cities counter the isolation of black kids from mainstream norms by making similar demands. They insist that their students learn how to speak standard English; show up on time, properly dressed; sit up straight at their desks, chairs pulled in, workbooks organized; never waste a minute in which they could be learning; walk down halls quickly and quietly; always finish their homework; look at people to whom they are talking; listen to teachers politely and follow their directions precisely; treat their classmates with respect; and shake hands with visitors to the school, introducing themselves.

The website of the Amistad Academy in New Haven contains a section called "Pillars of 'Harder and Smarter' Instruction." "Behavior," it explains, "should be thought of in the same way as academics—it must be taught. Effective behavioral instruction, like effective academic instruction, must be modeled, practiced, and reinforced."[17] At all good schools proper behavior is "modeled, practiced, and reinforced," and the messages about behavioral expectations are not add-ons, occasionally articulated by the principal or a teacher. They are part of an entire school culture, permeating every minute of the day. Moreover, even minor infractions of the rules—a shirt not tucked in, a bit of foul language—have immediate consequences. In 2005 the rules of basic business etiquette still apply, the president of a Massachusetts consulting firm told the *Boston Globe*. Stand up straight, look people in the eye, and be respectful and courteous.[18] Or, as journalist David Shipler has put it: "The 'soft skills' of punctuality, diligence, and a can-do attitude"—that is, internalized self-discipline and a belief that it will pay off—are as important as basic math skills.

"Are we conservative here?" Gregory Hodge, head of the Frederick Douglass Academy in New York's Harlem once asked me rhetorically. "Of course we are," he said. "We teach middle class values like responsibility." David Levin, founder of the KIPP Academy in the South Bronx, has echoed Hodge. "We are fighting a battle involving skills and values. We are not afraid to set social norms," he has said. The best schools work hard to instill the "desire, discipline, and dedication" (KIPP watchwords) that will enable disadvantaged youth to climb the American ladder of opportunity. The road to success is not paved with excuses—or second chances, Levin reminds his students.

Other, equally important messages permeate the culture of the schools. "Good things happen," KIPP's David Levin tells a class, letting the students finish the sentence, "when you do the right thing." When you make the right choices, in other words. It's an optimistic message about America and about the rules that govern the climb out of poverty to greater affluence. For those who make the right decisions, doors are open. Good schools do not promise a rose garden—a future in which race and ethnicity will not matter. Yet they suggest that the opportunities outweigh the barriers, that determination will pay off.

The effort to put disadvantaged youngsters on the traditional ladder of social mobility has another component, never explicitly articulated. The best inner-city schools demand that students choose to define themselves as individuals—just as they have chosen their education. They guide them down the road that Ralph Ellison walked seven decades ago. "In Macon County, Alabama," he wrote much later, "I read Marx, Freud, T. S. Eliot, Pound, Gertrude Stein and Hemingway. Books which seldom, if ever, mentioned Negroes were to release me from whatever 'segregated' idea I might have had of my human possibilities. I was freed not by propagandists ... but by composers, novelists, and poets who spoke to me of more interesting and freer ways of life."[19]

The notion of race as destiny, Ellison argued, stifles the development of individuality and nurtures "that feverish industry dedicated to telling Negroes who and what they are."[20] "If white society has tried to do anything to us," he noted in the 1970s, "it has tried to keep us from being individuals"—to deprive blacks of the understanding that "individuality is still operative beyond the racial structuring of American society."[21] The best schools try to teach children the lessons that Ellison had to figure out in terrible racial circumstances. They want their students to think of themselves as individuals "beyond the racial structuring of American society"—free to emphasize their racial and ethnic group ties as much or little as they wish. It's part of the culture of choice that these schools create—in sharp contrast to what is found throughout most of public education.

The Importance of Choice

As a goal, equality trumps freedom throughout most of American public education, with less equality as a result. Choice—for administrators, teachers, and students alike—is sacrificed on the altar of equity, and black children (America's most disadvantaged) are woefully left behind. Schools of education and public school teachers endlessly preach equality, but they defend a system that results in appalling racial disparities in learning.

The effort (waning but far from dead) to create racially balanced schools has assumed that more coercion will bring better education. And yet excellent inner-city schools that are meeting the needs of inner-city children are, of necessity, schools of choice. They cannot function unless principals have selected their staff, teachers have picked a school in which they belong, and families have chosen to send their children with the understanding that every hour of every day the students will be deciding whether to stay or go—whether to work hard and follow the rules or leave. Good preparation for life.

Absent choice, there is little sense of community, cohesion, teamwork, and real commitment. Only in a school in which people have chosen to work together can there be strict behavioral codes and social norms, as well as an insistence that students spend a high proportion of their waking hours learning. Think of the chaos in so many regular urban public schools. Conscripted students will often defeat a disciplined regimen to which they have given no assent.

Schools of choice can deliver basic messages about the rules of success in a fluid and open society in which individuals (whatever their color) in important ways are free to choose who they are, with the understanding that their choices will shape their lives. During the 2004 presidential campaign, Democratic nominee John Kerry told a predominantly black audience that the number of African Americans in prison was "unacceptable, but . . . not their fault."[22] His statement betrayed a profound disconnect from the values of choice and responsibility that most Americans embrace. Only when choice is built into the very structure of a school are those values integral to the educational culture and likely to be internalized by the students.

Almost all Americans now believe in racial equality, and good schools have become the key to that equality. And yet there are no excellent big-city school systems—not one is successfully turning around the lives of the inner-city kids who are tragically alienated from the world of learning. Only schools whose mission is both academic and cultural can hope to succeed in such a transforming project. But that dual mission cannot be accomplished except in schools in which choice permeates the educational culture.

Notes

1. Richard Rothstein, *Class and Schools: Using Social, Economic, and Educational Reform to Close the Black-White Achievement Gap* (Washington: Economic Policy Institute, 2004), pp. 39, 129, 131.

2. See, for example, Larry V. Hedges and Amy Nowell, "Black-White Test Score Convergence since 1965," in *The Black-White Test Score Gap*, ed. Christopher Jencks and Meredith Phillips (Washington: Brookings Institution Press, 1998), chap. 5. The literature on social class as the explanation for the gap is reviewed in Abigail Thernstrom and Stephan Thernstrom, *No Excuses: Closing the Racial Gap in Learning* (New York: Simon & Schuster, 2003), pp. 124–30.

3. Rothstein, pp. 133, 135.

4. See Thernstrom and Thernstrom, chaps. 8–10.

5. A 1995 survey of 103 urban school districts found that 45 percent were under court order to maintain racially balanced schools; for the large districts the figure was 69 percent. Many more had voluntarily adopted some sort of desegregation program. Council of Urban Boards of Education, *Still Separate, Still Unequal? Desegregation in the 1990s* (Alexandria, VA: National School Boards Association, 1995), pp. 19, 26–27.

6. Not all busing plans were court ordered; some were adopted by public officials, and others masqueraded as voluntary but were, in fact, coerced by policies like that in Massachusetts that tied state funding for school construction to a desegregation plan. But a vast majority were the consequence of judicial action.

7. Quoted in Ronald P. Formisano, *Boston against Busing: Race, Class, and Ethnicity in the 1960s and 1970s* (Chapel Hill: University of North Carolina Press, 1991), p. 193. Everyone understands that busing was wildly unpopular among whites, but few know that surveys in the decade 1972 to 1982 indicated that busing was favored by only a slight majority of black parents. Howard Schuman, Charlotte Steen, and Lawrence Bobo, *Racial Attitudes in America: Trends and Interpretations* (Cambridge, MA: Harvard University Press, 1985), pp. 144–47. These are figures from the National Opinion Research Center. Polls by another leading organization, the Institute for Social Research, in 1972, 1974, 1976, and 1980 showed that only in 1976 did a majority of blacks (57 percent) approve busing. In the other three years, the results were 46 percent, 43 percent, and 49 percent. Not very impressive backing from a group in whose name the litigation that resulted in the busing orders was undertaken.

8. Gary Orfield, "Schools More Separate: Consequences of a Decade of Resegregation," Harvard Civil Rights Project, July 2001. This report is only one of many that Orfield has written making basically the same points.

9. This argument is spelled out in Thernstrom and Thernstrom. See especially, chap. 9.

10. Experts in a case involving a challenge to the Lynn, Massachusetts, desegregation plan "described numerous educational benefits derived from Lynn's plan. These

include improved racial tolerance, more effective preparation for living and working in an increasingly multi-racial world, higher attendance rates, lower suspension rates, and safer school environments." Nancy McCardle and Anne Wheelock, "Should Lynn Schools Use Boston Model?" op-ed, *Boston Globe*, December 18, 2004. Note the absence of any reference to improved academic performance.

11. College Board, *Reaching the Top: A Report of the National Task Force on Minority Achievement* (Washington: U.S. Department of Labor, 1999), pp. 7, 14, 17, 18.

12. See, e.g., Laurence Steinberg, *Beyond the Classroom: Why School Reform Has Failed and What Parents Need to Do* (New York: Simon & Schuster, 1996).

13. Martin Luther King Jr., Speech in Chicago, 1963, as quoted in Shelby Steele, *The Content of Our Character: A New Vision of Race in America* (New York: St. Martin's, 1990), p. 138. Ronald Ferguson has used the same metaphor: "After all, no runner ever came from behind by running the same speed as race leaders." Ronald Ferguson, "Addressing Racial Disparities in High-Achieving Suburban Schools," *Policy Issues* (North Central Regional Educational Laboratory), no. 13 (November 2002): 4.

14. Pedro A. Noguera, "Racial Politics and the Elusive Quest for Excellent and Equity in Education," *Education and Urban Society* 34 (November 2001): 18–41; and Pedro A. Noguera, "The Trouble with Black Boys," *Harvard Journal of African Americans and Public Policy* 3 (Fall 2001): 23–46.

15. Orlando Patterson, "What to Do When Busing Becomes Irrelevant," *New York Times*, July 18, 1999, p. 17.

16. Thomas Sowell, *Black Rednecks and White Liberals* (San Francisco: Encounter Books, 2005), pp. 35–37.

17. www.amistadacademy.org/about.modelschool.behavior.html.

18. Kate M. Jackson, "Minding Your Manners Still Matters," *Boston Globe*, May 29, 2005.

19. Ralph Ellison, "The World and the Jug," in *The Collected Essays of Ralph Ellison*, ed. John F. Callahan (New York: Modern Library, 1995), p. 164.

20. Ralph Ellison, "The Shadow and the Act," in *Collected Essays*, p. 57.

21. Ralph Ellison "Indivisible Man," first published in 1970, in *Collected Essays*, p. 394; and "'A Completion of Personality': A Talk with Ralph Ellison," *Collected Essays*, p. 799.

22. Quoted in Charles Hurt, "Kerry Woos Middle Class," *Washington Times*, June 17, 2004.

4. Milton Friedman, Vouchers, and Civic Values

Jay P. Greene

Many people are willing to accept that vouchers would improve educational achievement, but they worry about how choice, especially choice involving religiously affiliated schools, might affect the health of our democracy. The "civic values" case against school choice is that government-operated schools help to ensure that future generations learn political tolerance and other civic values, whereas privately operated schools might promote divisiveness or intolerance or otherwise undermine the civic values necessary for the proper functioning of our political system. Opponents of vouchers usually assume that they are the only ones focusing on this issue and believe that supporters of choice largely ignore civic concerns and focus instead on academic achievement. That assumption is not borne out when we examine the seminal work that started the school choice movement: Milton Friedman's 1955 piece, "The Role of Government in Education."

Distorted Readings

Friedman's 1955 essay is almost entirely concerned with the importance of education in protecting "a stable and democratic society" and whether "denationalization" of education with vouchers would undermine that stable democracy. Unfortunately, that is seldom how Friedman's writing on school choice is described. People who believe that supporters of vouchers are largely uninterested in the effects of school choice on civic values seem to have ignored Friedman's seminal article on the subject, or at least have failed to understand what it said.

Amy Gutmann, author of the widely read book, *Democratic Education*, is representative of the typical interpretation of Friedman's voucher proposal. Gutmann correctly quotes Friedman as proposing that the government role in education be limited "to assuring that

49

the schools [meet] certain minimum standards such as the inclusion of a minimum content in their programs, much as it now inspects restaurants to assure that they maintain minimum sanitary standards." She wrongly suggests, however, that Friedman's concerns do not extend beyond "preventing schools from physically harming children or fraudulently claiming to educate them." She even describes Friedman as arguing "that educating citizens is a side effect, rather than a central purpose . . . of schooling."[1] More recently, political scientist Kevin Smith, writing a review of research on vouchers, made the following claim: "Even prochoice theorists concede that programs allowing complete freedom can produce racially, religiously, or socio-economically segregated schools."[2] To support his claim, Smith provides the following citation: "See, for example, Friedman 1955."

What Friedman Actually Says

It is difficult to see how anyone could actually read his 1955 article and come away with the idea that Friedman was unconcerned with the effects of education on civic values or that he was conceding that vouchers would cause segregation. The first main section of the article is subtitled "General Education for Citizenship," and here Friedman begins by noting that "a stable and democratic society is impossible without widespread acceptance of some common set of values."[3] Friedman then goes on to consider the argument that, without government operation of schools, "it might . . . be impossible to provide the common core of values deemed requisite for social stability."[4] Friedman takes the threat vouchers potentially pose to civic values seriously, noting that "this argument has considerable force." He also considers the possibility that vouchers would "exacerbate class distinctions" or be used "as a means of evading the Supreme Court ruling against segregation."[5] The idea that vouchers might facilitate segregation causes Friedman to devote to the issue a page-long footnote in which he concedes that "my initial reaction—and I venture to predict, that of most readers—was that this possible use of the proposal was a count against it, that it was a particularly striking case of the possible defect—the exacerbating of class distinctions."[6]

Friedman gives serious consideration to all of those concerns, and he also makes a powerful case for how vouchers might not only preserve freedom but actually enhance civic values. First, Friedman observes that instilling a common set of values to preserve a democratic system might in itself produce "indoctrination inhibiting freedom of thought and belief." Suggesting the necessity of careful discernment in such matters, Friedman observes that the line between what is necessary for common social values and what is excessive in inhibiting freedom "is another of those vague boundaries that is easier to mention that to define."[7]

Second, Friedman speculates that vouchers might enhance civic values by reducing demand for religiously affiliated schools, which had come to be perceived as the most significant potential threat to tolerance and civic values. Under the status quo, Friedman observes, parental options are largely limited to free government-operated schools and subsidized parochial schools. But with vouchers "a wide variety of schools will spring up to meet the demand," including a large number of secular schools. To the extent that parochial schools posed the greatest threat of sectarian conflict, expanding the range of affordable options to include secular schools might produce "less rather than more parochial education" and enhance social stability.[8]

Third, Friedman rejects the concern that vouchers would exacerbate segregation. He observes that "under the present arrangements, particular schools tend to be peopled by children with similar backgrounds thanks to the stratification of residential areas." He further observes that people with higher incomes can more easily afford private school tuition, artificially exaggerating the lack of diversity in public schools. By detaching schooling from housing and by reducing the financial barriers to attending private school, vouchers "would operate to reduce both kinds of stratification."[9]

Friedman pays special attention to the possible use of vouchers to evade the Supreme Court ruling against racial segregation in schools, devoting another page-long footnote to the issue. He makes clear that he is just as opposed to making vouchers available only for students who attend segregated schools, which had been proposed in some southern states, as he is to legally segregated public schools. The solution, he suggests, is universally to offer parents vouchers and allow them to seek segregated or desegregated schools according to their own preferences while trying to persuade parents of the virtues of sending their children to integrated schools. Although he declares that he personally deplores "segregation and racial prejudice," he recognizes that others believe differently and may choose segregated schools.[10] Friedman argues that the principle of individual freedom requires that those choices be permitted. Implicit in his argument, however, is the faith that not too many people are likely to choose segregated schools, at least not enough to threaten the widespread acceptance and understanding of the civic values necessary for a stable democracy.

What Recent Empirical Research Has Shown

In his 1955 essay, all of Friedman's arguments are supported by reference to logic, theory, and principle rather than empirical analysis. It is impressive, then, that the empirical work that has been done over the last five decades gives considerable support to Friedman's predictions about the effects of school choice on civic values. In particular, the evidence suggests that universal implementation of vouchers would enhance political tolerance as well as reduce school segregation.

Political Tolerance

To measure political tolerance, social scientists have developed a technique that is widely accepted in the field. Subjects are asked to name their least-liked group, sometimes from a list of groups provided. People most often pick the Ku Klux Klan, American Nazis, Communists, gay activists, or the religious right. Subjects are then asked how willing they would be to let members of their least-liked group engage in political activities, such as run for elective office or hold a rally in their town. The more willing people are to let their least-liked group engage in political activities, the more tolerant they are said to be.

Patrick Wolf of Georgetown University recently conducted a systematic review of research on the effects of private schooling on political tolerance. He identified 12 studies containing 18 analyses that compare the political tolerance produced by public and private schooling in the United States. Ten of the 18 analyses show that private education has statistically significant benefits for political tolerance, seven analyses produce statistically insignificant results, and one analysis finds that public education has significantly better results for political tolerance. The pattern of research results clearly supports the notion that expanding access to private schools with vouchers would more likely strengthen than diminish political tolerance. At the very least, it is safe to say that the empirical evidence provides little support for the claim that vouchers would undermine desirable civic values.[11]

Such positive effects of private schooling are not associated, as Friedman theorized they might be, only with attendance at secular private schools. In one study I conducted with Nicole Mellow and Joseph Giammo at the University of Texas, we examined the effect of private school education on the political tolerance of a nationally representative sample of adult Latinos. Despite the fact that nearly all of the private schools attended by Latinos were Catholic schools, private school education appears to have contributed to political tolerance later in life. That result is even more striking when one considers that gay activists were the least-liked group most commonly selected by Latinos. The more Catholic school the Latinos in our sample attended, the more tolerant they were of the political rights of gay activists.[12]

There are several possible explanations for the tolerance-promoting effects of secular and religious private schools. First, instructional effectiveness may benefit political tolerance just as it does academic achievement. Private schools may more effectively convey civic values just as they tend to more effectively convey math or reading skills. Second, because public schools are politically governed, they may be more likely to avoid politically controversial topics even if effective teaching of political tolerance requires that those topics be discussed candidly. Perhaps fear of offending a political constituency deters public schools from having open and honest discussions about the political activities of gays, racial minorities, or other groups, whereas private schools feel more empowered to address those issues. In other words, "political correctness" in public schools may actually undermine political tolerance. Third, parochial schools may not be particularly threatening to civic values because they may effectively distinguish between their moral judgments about certain activities and people's political rights to engage in those activities. In their own parlance, parochial schools may teach students to hate the sin without hating the sinner. Finally, in the case of parochial schools in particular, it may be that there is an underlying philosophical commitment to the civic values of tolerance and freedom that protect religious minorities from prosecution and persecution.

Although the empirical evidence does not allow us to determine the extent to which those or other factors explain positive effects of private education on political tolerance, it clearly supports the existence of those positive effects.

Racial Segregation

Empirical evidence also clearly supports the positive effect of private education on reducing racial segregation. As Friedman theorized, it appears that public schools perpetuate and perhaps reinforce racial segregation in housing. Private schools, on the other hand, are able to draw students from across school district and attendance zone boundaries, producing somewhat less segregated learning environments.

In an analysis I conducted of the racial composition of 12th-grade classrooms using data from the National Education Longitudinal Study, private school students were significantly less likely to be in classrooms that were racially segregated than were public school students. More than half (55 percent) of the students in public schools were in classrooms in which more than 90 percent of the students were white or in which more than 90 percent were racial minorities. Fewer than half (41 percent) of private school students were in similarly segregated classrooms. Levels of segregation are quite high in both the public and the private sector, but the problem is less extensive in private schools.[13]

In another study I conducted with Nicole Mellow we examined the extent of racial integration in public and private school lunchrooms in two Texas cities. We observed that 64 percent of private school students were sitting in racially mixed groups in the cafeteria, with at least one student adjacent to or across from a student of a different racial or ethnic background, compared to 50 percent of public school students. After adjusting for the size of the schools, the grade level of students, and the existence of seating restrictions, we found that 79 percent of private school students sit in racially mixed groups at lunch compared to 43 percent of public school students. One is much more likely to observe the voluntary mixing of students from different racial backgrounds in private school lunchrooms. That is racial integration where the rubber hits the road, where education can really affect social harmony.[14]

Would those positive effects of private education on reducing segregation continue if access to private schools was expanded to the broader public with vouchers? Early evidence from school choice programs in Milwaukee and Cleveland suggests that it would. In Milwaukee, Howard Fuller of Marquette University and Deborah Greiveldinger, then of the American Education Reform Council, compared the extent of segregation in public schools and private schools participating in the city's voucher program. They found that 54 percent of Milwaukee public school students attended racially segregated schools, compared to 50 percent of students at private schools receiving voucher students. The likelihood of being in a segregated school dropped to 42 percent for voucher students who chose religiously affiliated private schools.[15]

I found the same pattern in a study I conducted of the effect of Cleveland's voucher program on the likelihood that students would attend a racially segregated school. I found that 61 percent of students in the Cleveland metropolitan area attended segregated schools where more than 90 percent of students were white or more than 90 percent were of minority backgrounds and 50 percent of students attended private schools with vouchers. Although the difference was not dramatic, the probability of attending a segregated school was higher if a student was in a public school than if a student attended a private school with a voucher.[16]

Longevity of an Idea

We may readily conclude that Milton Friedman's theoretical case for the benefits of vouchers for civic education has stood the test of time. His 1955 discussion of the potential threats vouchers pose to democratic stability, as well as his logical refutation of those threats, is as relevant and persuasive as it would be had it been written yesterday rather than five decades ago. Moreover, the empirical evidence that has been collected in recent years provides considerable support for Friedman's half-century-old arguments.

It should come as little surprise that opponents of vouchers are woefully ignorant of Friedman's concern for and insights on the effects of vouchers on civic values. Many of those people have a visceral reaction to the mention of Milton Friedman that blinds them to what he has to say on the topic. Some think that they already know what Friedman has to say, even if they haven't read more than the few sentences from his original article that are commonly cited by critics and recycled in subsequent pieces by others. Many opponents of school choice thus simply assume that Friedman lacks interest in civic education and focuses solely on how competition improves academic achievement. If they actually read the article in full, those opponents would be surprised to discover that Friedman devotes almost his entire discussion of K–12 education to a consideration of the effects of vouchers on democratic stability.

Somewhat more surprising is how little supporters of vouchers know about Friedman's thinking on vouchers and civic values. Many strong advocates of school choice tend to assume that Friedman, like many of them, is mostly concerned with competition and educational efficiency. They, too, would benefit enormously from actually reading the article that sparked the modern interest in vouchers.

Notes

1. Amy Gutmann, *Democratic Education* (Princeton, NJ: Princeton University Press, 1987), pp. 67–68.

2. Kevin Smith, "Data Don't Matter? Academic Research and School Choice," *Perspectives on Politics,* June 2005, p. 292.

3. Milton Friedman, "The Role of Government in Education," in *Economics and the Public Interest,* ed. Robert A. Solo (New Brunswick, NJ: Rutgers University Press, 1955), p. 124.

4. Ibid., p. 128.

5. Ibid., pp. 129–31.

6. Ibid., p. 131.

7. Ibid., p. 129.

8. Ibid.

9. Ibid., p. 130.

10. Ibid., p. 131.

11. Patrick J. Wolf, "School Choice and Civic Values," in *Getting Choice Right,* ed. Julian R. Betts and Tom Loveless (Washington: Brookings Institution Press, 2006).

12. Jay P. Greene, Nicole Mellow, and Joseph Giammo, "The Effect of Private Education on Political Participation, Social Capital and Tolerance: An Examination of the Latino National Political Survey," *Georgetown Public Policy Review* 5, no. 1 (Fall 1999).

13. Jay P. Greene, "Civic Values in Public and Private Schools," in *Learning from School Choice,* ed. Paul Peterson and Bryan Hassel (Washington: Brookings Institution Press, 1998).

14. Jay P. Greene and Nicole Mellow, "Integration Where It Counts," *Texas Education Review* 5, no. 1 (Spring 2000).

15. Howard Fuller and Deborah Greiveldinger, "The Impact of School Choice on Racial Integration in Milwaukee Private Schools," American Education Reform Council, unpublished manuscript, 2002.

16. Greene.

5. Give Us Liberty and Give Us Depth

John E. Coons

I have known Milton Friedman for 40 years and relish the opportunity to reflect on his legacy. My admiration for the man is quite undiminished by our brisk and ongoing debate over liberty's specific place in the vindication of parental choice.

The country is grateful for its good and gifted classical economists. Together they have delivered the wisdom of the market in terms we could understand. Half a century ago, they sailed bravely upstream, Milton Friedman in the vanguard. Just when needed, Friedman—and most especially he—was there to warn America of the free lunch and remind us of the benign uses of competition. Whether the immediate object of his attention was money, meat, mortgages, or the military, he was right. I am personally in his intellectual debt. Citizens like me listened and learned, then together we untethered the banks, the airlines, and the supermarkets—and grew surprisingly rich.

Ordinary Americans have found free-market ideology a potion intoxicating yet wholesome. And it is no criticism that a tonic so healing could be intellectually delicate, as I will now respectfully suggest. On rare occasions, like the best of wines, this creed does not travel well. In the case of schooling, it was destined, at least so far, not to travel at all. Though here and there choice now emerges as school policy, it has succeeded principally by holding the familiar maxims of the market at arms length. And nothing resembling Friedman's ideal structure has become law.

That is not all bad, but it is odd and deserves remark. Certainly, Friedman has been right all along to suppose that America needs to subsidize choice and to remake schooling into a market that includes all players, particularly parents. It puzzles, then, that his form of the message has proved so unwelcome among a public otherwise enthusiastic for tales of Adam Smith. After all, it was that sort of plain argument from pure liberty that brought us food stamps, housing vouchers, and liberation from medical bondage at the county hospital. But, again and again, when applied to schools, it failed to move more than a third of the voters. In the 1980s and 1990s, eight statewide referenda, all of them cast in pure market form and paraded in its familiar imagery, were sent to their doom— with what delay and damage to the hope for choice is for the historian to assess.

In the meantime, it fell to a mix of maverick politicians in Wisconsin to make parental choice real by giving its classical lines an extreme makeover; in their hands the thing was transformed into a targeted preference for the poor, a device of the baroque and bastard sort that Friedman had repeatedly and successfully opposed in California (as he puts it, "any program for the poor is a poor program"). The Milwaukee device was sold, not with the tropes of individualism, but with a package of specific practical outcomes ranging from fiscal frugality to law and order to the dignity of teachers—and even to the hope of racial integration. Of course, naked market theory received its fair share of airtime, but the Wisconsin audience was allowed to see its claims in context and to appreciate economic liberty more as an instrument to secure a menagerie of public and private goods—and less as an end in itself. The prevalence of that Milwaukee mindset has now been confirmed in state after state plus the District of Columbia, while the focused individualist message continues to fare so badly that friends of choice implore its apostles to cease and desist. Perhaps it is time to adjust the style if not the substance of the crusade that this volume is intended to witness and honor.

The problem is twofold: we need to be more precise about the nature and locus of the various freedoms that are experienced or intended in the choice of a school, and we should never allow those freedoms to appear to be the only values at stake. I will address these issues in order.

The champion of school choice who intends the outcome to be something more than an academic exercise eventually comes to terms with the reality that the central ideas of market individualism bear obscurely on the complex of relationships that we call school. To the enthusiast, that can come as a surprise. Embarked on his historic mission to pulverize yet another bloated monopoly, the economist-liberator sails straight into a Bermuda Triangle of confounding ideologies. The classical images of economics are not unwelcome here, but, in the context of schooling, they find themselves confronting other conceptions, both powerful and exotic, that lurk within the equally enigmatic triangle of parent, child, and state. The clear market message that steered us through the reform of communications and monetary policy here becomes an erratic compass. Instinct assures us that schooling can benefit from operating as a market, but our arguments for that claim can no longer proceed as if the actors were fungible; to the contrary, their roles are subtle and diverse, and there is more at stake than an abstract buyer getting his goods at lower prices from an abstract seller. In fact, in the relation called school, the very identification of the buyer becomes a puzzle, making a jumble of our reliance on personal freedom.

Happily, this elemental confusion is at last beginning to dissipate, at least in those quarters where insight is likely to count in the making of policy. One by one, from the timid cloisters of the political middle, new players are emerging to support school choice. They too value liberty and the market, but they are able to see that school is something more and different. As did Friedman in his earlier battles with Leviathan, these contemporaries deserve our encouragement. The most useful first step might be a reform of the vocabulary available to new players as they address the public mind. The shift should not be all that difficult.

It will begin with that plain fact of nature that makes the school market different from those for shoes and insurance: under no circumstances can the child himself be "free to choose"; necessarily the decision will be that of some adult whom we will empower by law and public subsidy. Subsidized school choice is a policy by which the state facilitates a temporary sovereignty of one particular human over another. Before we evangelize in the name of "freedom," we must face up to the incongruity of attaching that term to such a relationship. If we truly want change driven by rationality, we will adopt an idiom that keeps the language of liberty under some restraint. I worry at the metaphors used by the very institution that Milton Friedman established to carry the banner for the idea of school choice. On the desk before me, as I write, rests the Friedman Foundation's long litany of "freedoms," broadcast in a dazzling new brochure and culminating with the ecstatic "This Is Freedom; This Is School Choice."

The unnuanced claim of freedom can be awkward and politically risky. Sheer power over somebody else could, I suppose, be called a form of freedom. But I doubt that even the most ardent libertarian would be content to have school choice understood simply as a license from government for one person to dominate another; indeed such a usage would as aptly describe the power that is now exercised by the school bureaucrat. For him, too, "this is school choice"—it is authority and power bestowed upon an adult to conscript Susie Smith for the Horace Mann School. That authority could even be represented in a voucher that is to be spent by an agent of the state on Susie in a school of the agent's choice.

Domination, then, is simply part of the architecture of school choice, as it is of the rest of childhood. However, that reality does not eliminate freedom either as a fact peculiar to the adult or as a hope peculiar to the child. The use of the terms "freedom" and "liberty," even in this context of domination, will be warranted or inappropriate according to the particular office and purpose of the adult who competes for the power to decide. For the agent of the state, the purpose of a child's assignment to a school is already fixed by law. The meaning of his own act of choice has been prescribed; even if he enjoys a certain discretion, it is a ministerial responsibility and not bestowed to serve some purpose of his own. That holds even where the declared legislated objective is the eventual autonomy of the individual child (the second species of freedom that I will consider below); for, again, freedom entails mastery of purpose. Nor can the word apply to the ruling legislative act, portraying it as a freedom of the state itself. That would fail as a simple confusion of categories; at least in this context, freedom implies the will of some natural person.

In the case of school choice, the only adult person who is in a position to experience such a liberty of office and purpose in the act of choice is the parent. Like the bureaucrat, the parent dominates the child; but, unlike the bureaucrat or any other adult, it is she who determines the end of her choices. She is the master of their meaning for the child and—in all but the choice to abuse—for society as well. It may be tough news for John Dewey, but she is boss. Moreover, her vast discretion proceeds, not from mere governmental authority, but from something more—from sources secure against any design of the state to disenfranchise. It precedes the Constitution itself in order of time and has long been conceded by judges to constitute a distinct order of authority over the individual child. Apart from cases of utter incapacity or wickedness, mother and father are legislator, executive, and judge.

In its authority over the meaning and practice of the good life for this child the cluster of parental powers also stands as one of those intellectual and moral claims that command unique gravitas in both political culture and positive law. Choice is the stuff of First Amendment concern quite apart from the invocation of religious freedom. Far from being an exercise of naked domination, then, the parent's role can be, and ordinarily is, one of responsible freedom. Whether or not we can discover in this relationship a second form of freedom for the child, for the parent freedom is a fact.

Note that the parent's freedom is experienced as an act of personal expression that is addressed to two distinct audiences. One is the child who is to embrace and practice its content; the parent has chosen this school as her intellectual agent to deliver her own worldview to Susie. The second audience is the rest of us—the world if you will. The parent aims to embody her message in this child who will in time go forth as the family's ambassador to the generations. I think these are the sorts of meanings that we intend when we speak of parental freedom. Again, like any freedom, that of parents can be neglected or even abused and descend into license; and I do not deny the state's role as rescue team. These few distinctions do not do justice to the idea of parental freedom, but gradually we who value choice and carry its banner must learn to do so.

I turn now to focus on that other authentic liberty that is unique to the child. Adult domination—whether by parent or state—can, and generally does, seek the eventual autonomy of the child as one of its objectives. The chances for this objective to be realized in any particular child will be affected by the exercise of authority here and now by some grownup. The child's liberated maturity, if it comes, will do so in some part either because of, or in spite of, this temporary condition of dependence and subordination. I would add parenthetically that the nurture of the child's autonomy is, in this culture, widely understood not only as a goal proper to the dominating adult but as a responsibility.

Once we discern the child's own ultimate freedom as a separate value, we are in a better position to assess parental choice of school as its efficient instrument. But as we make this intelligible claim for the family (as I have often done), let us be aware that it carries an intellectual and political risk. Specifically, it invites a riposte in kind from the government school establishment. Yes, says the old guard, the child's ultimate autonomy is a goal, and we professionals must in all justice promote it. Like you economists, we schoolmasters feel bad that the present regime must treat the ordinary family as if it were feckless and irresponsible. This is undemocratic to be sure, but a cost to be borne. For, sadly, there is truth to the vague fear that to facilitate the exercise of choice by common folks would be to reduce rather than encourage the autonomy of their children. On balance, then, it is a consolation that America's disenfranchisement of have-not families works to the long-range benefit of their children. For the liberation of Susie Smith lies in her assignment to P. S. 202 instead of the sort of school that might be preferred by her not-so-sophisticated parents.

Of course, this sort of defense of the status quo—that government does it better—is not kept in special reserve to rebut only those arguments that are made in the name of a child's liberty. The state educator will respond the same way to every claim that the extension of choice will produce some plausible benefit, whether it be freedom or better health. Whatever one might propose as a true and proper aim of schooling—from higher scores to lower crime rates—will be met with an assertion that, at least in the case of the poor, this particular worthy objective is best served by a school assignment that is compulsory and a curriculum that is uniform; if you have some benign aspiration for schools, the government professional will be its best champion. It is on that ground that some educators regret that public schools in this society lack the authority to impose the same saving experiences on the children of the rich. What we have is second best. Still, working within these restraints, we professionals do our best; and insofar as the specific object is the child's ultimate autonomy, it is government that knows how to attain it. Public school will liberate those young conscripts who were lucky enough to get themselves born to the poor. If liberty is your concern, that is the state educators' answer.

It is my impression that—when thus limited to the goal of the child's eventual independence—this answer from the public schoolmaster seems plausible to many American citizens. More, it can hold true in individual cases. For reasons that include the specific risk that they pose to their own child's ultimate autonomy, the state disempowers the occasional feckless or brutal parents; they forfeit the authority to decide about the school along with every other choice affecting the child's welfare. The practical question is this: can these adults whom we must reluctantly disenfranchise be identified en masse as members of an economic class, as is now the policy of the schools? Are the middle class okay and the poor incompetent? As we confront that broad issue, we begin to see that the child's eventual autonomy is only one among many concerns in a much more general inquiry about the best decider for Susie. The same question of the right adult to govern the young person will arise separately with respect to every legitimate purpose—private and public—that could be affected by the choice of school. Will coercion by government or by the parent be more effective at achieving each of those objectives?

To encourage civic discourse about the many particular, sometimes merely utilitarian, implications of choice is not to deny what I have said of the distinctive liberties at stake here. The free responsibility of the parent to set the child's compass is an end in itself, one confirmed by nature, convention, positive law, and—for my part— higher authority. Absent serious abuse, its invulnerability holds whether the parent does or does not succeed in enhancing the child's own liberty, or indeed, as with the Amish, even when the parents positively reject the notion of autonomy as a meaningless vanity. The point is not that the parent always makes the choice that, to the liberty-minded, would seem best for the child, but that, for many a good reason, she is simply the best to make it.

In any case, it is intellectually and politically prudent to assert, if it be true, that parental choice implicates not only the welfare of the child but also various aspects of the common good of the sort constantly, and successfully, paraded by professional educators. People do care about cost, security, social harmony, ideological diversity, religious values, racial integration, and even that permanent obsession of the educated—test scores. If choice ever does arrive for the poor, it will be because these publicly valued outcomes have been adequately vetted for and by the voters, as they were in Wisconsin.

Seeing this we begin to appreciate the risk in any obsessive reliance on the imperative of freedom—whether for child, parent, or both. Yes, there is a strong argument to be made that a general policy of parental choice has the best chance to maximize Susie's ultimate autonomy. And, if we argued nothing but this one claim, we would no doubt persuade a significant number of those citizens whose primary hope from education politics is a system that delivers every child to an adult status rich in raw opportunity—both objective and subjective. I personally believe that broad parental authority is the proper instrument for attaining the particular end labeled the child's "autonomy"—however that is conceived. The National Education Association has it wrong. One day we might win that argument with the public.

Or we might not. The voices for choice that have sung no song but the hymn to liberty have so little to show for all their money. The great center of the American electorate remains unmoved. It could be that, for most people, the liberation of the ordinary family as advertised is only one objective among many to be served by schooling; hence, even if choice were to win the focused argument about the proper path to liberty of child as well as parent, it would face a dozen others about something else that bothers the citizen. And it may be that the parent will not emerge as the obvious instrument of every hope for the common good. Family choice might not, for instance, be the best instrument for somebody's objective of maximizing public expenditure on education (though I have long argued that it is); and it might not encourage uniformity in curriculum so well as those "standards" that could emerge from the No Child Left Behind Act (and for this, bravo). But to address all such difficult and relevant questions and to work them through one by one is the very point of civic discourse. Hence, if one specific goal were racial integration, we would together consider whether the school choices of low-income parents in the District of Columbia or Kansas City would be likely to help or hurt (a no brainer). Or, if the concern be that schools should nurture social trust among have-nots, we would ask whether the display of civic confidence that is represented in school choice for ordinary parents would be repaid in kind or would, on balance, increase social faction.

A strong concern of my own is the integrity of the family itself. This is another bedrock social good that is difficult to analyze in the argot of individual liberty, because it is about so much more than liberty. It entails the (temporary) authority and responsibility of fathers and mothers and, correspondingly, the child's vocation of obedience. We know the meaning of choice for middle-class parents who are in a position to exercise it; much more than a mere satisfaction of somebody's market preference, their choice of school expresses the very identity of the family as it strives to preserve itself. But, in my experience, primordial group insight of this sort has rarely been featured in the discourse of the focused libertarian. Assessment of the social worth of specific outcomes has not been his department.

In his role as citizen he should make it so, if only to preserve the subject of Friedman's original vision. The very idea of school choice assumes the vitality of this always unique cluster—this "little commonwealth"—whose members will, by nature and society, be accountable in their own lives for the results of the education of one specific child. And there could be no policy more deadly to that assumption than today's message from the government to the urban parent that, once Susie reaches age five, family becomes untrusted by society—a fossil thing unnecessary and powerless. One sometimes hears, in a perversity of language, that, under the present school regime, the unfortunate parent is liberated from an intolerable burden and receives a measure of freedom. If so, it is a liberation to emptiness. What she needs is not a further reminder of her worst possibilities but, rather, an invitation to dignity through authority and responsibility. And Susie desperately needs to witness these qualities in her parents.

She deserves a reason to believe that family can be a powerful, authoritative guiding institution—that there is an alternative to the present servile experience of the urban poor. Mr. Bill Cosby blames the family for the current reality, and he has reason. But its prostration may be a reality to which the conscriptive public school has contributed in a profound and poisonous way. If this be true, as we argue for choice, it will be important to say so.

I have no reason to think that either Milton Friedman or any of his collaborators is insensitive to such practical social consequences of empowering the poor. Indeed, I know otherwise. But the quality of argumentation has not yet risen to the dignity of the subject. The enchantment of high economic theory has lured many fine minds away from the main event that must take place, not only in that rare atmosphere of theory, but in the parliament of pedestrian concerns about the common good and the welfare of real children. These are subjects that do not always compute well in the coin of pure liberty. And so I say devoutly: thank you —and let us all keep on thinking.

6. Is There Hope for Expanded School Choice?

Eric A. Hanushek

Because they are products of circumstance, ideas often become dated. As circumstances change, many ideas lose currency and relevance. Others, however, pick up momentum with time. School choice is among the latter.

Over a long period of time, various philosophers, writers, and policymakers have discussed how schools should be organized and financed, but perhaps no idea about schooling is as directly linked to a single individual as school choice is to Milton Friedman. His proposal for educational vouchers was first put on paper in 1955, and it was included in his 1962 classic, *Capitalism and Freedom*, a broader introduction to the connections between economic freedom and political freedom. Of his insights into a number of government functions in modern societies, none was more powerful than his discussion of education.

The Context

The expansion of schooling during the 20th century dramatically changed the nature of discussions about education in America. The United States, which led the world's educational transformation, saw its largely private, locally run school system expand dramatically in both breadth and depth. Just as elementary schooling had become universal during the 19th century, so did secondary schooling become the norm during the 20th.

The 20th century also saw a dramatic consolidation of school districts. In 1937 there were 119,000 separate public school districts. Today there are fewer than 15,000.[1] Over the same period, funding of education also changed dramatically. In 1930 less than one-half percent of revenues for elementary and secondary schools came from the federal government, and less than one-fifth came from states, leaving over 80 percent to be raised locally. By 2000 the local share was down to 43 percent and both federal and state shares were rising.[2]

Taking those trends together, it is reasonable to assume that parents were much closer to what was going on in the schools 75 years ago than they are today. Likewise, school administrators in the small districts of the past, supported largely by local funds, almost certainly paid closer attention to the needs and desires of the families they served. School district consolidation has effectively moved decisionmaking about and management of education away from the local population. Moreover, larger districts with larger populations mean that there are more diverse preferences among parents for what they want in their schools. Thus, the administration of any district necessarily requires compromises among the various interests.

The influence of parents and local administrators has also changed because of the overall centralization of decisionmaking that has been occurring over the past century. As states have become more prominent in the funding of schools, they have also moved toward more centralized decisionmaking about the operations of schools. That is understandable because, if states are going to fund schools, they have responsibilities not to waste their (or the federal government's) funds. The overall result of the trends in government revenue and administration of education is that school decisions have migrated away from parents and local voters and toward state bureaucracies.

The experience of Americans with the small school districts prevalent at the beginning of the last century is one model of effective school organization. Schools can be responsive to their constituencies if the schools deal with a limited number of parents and if the parents directly control the funding of the schools.

A somewhat different view appeared in academic writing in the middle of the 20th century. Charles Tiebout acknowledged the persistent desires of parents for greater influence in local schools (or public services in general) but didn't believe that responsiveness of districts would have to be restored through direct consultation with all of the parents. Tiebout suggested that parents could satisfy their desires for local governmental services by shopping for the jurisdiction that provided the services that best met their individual desires. Thus, by living in the same area, parents with similar desires could group together to ensure more homogeneous demands. Moreover, since one aspect of schools involves how effectively they use their resources, competition for consumers could put competitive pressures on school districts to improve their performance and efficiency.[3]

The idea of shopping across alternative jurisdictions does, however, have limitations. Specifically, it requires that there be a large number of districts so that there is a sufficient range of choice. It also becomes very complicated when parents have multiple interests. For example, some parents may, in addition to schools, have desires with respect to welfare payments, hospital coverage, police, and safety. Selection of place of residence on the basis of school districts may compete with or fail to satisfy the other interests of the family.

A significant percentage of housing decisions involves finding a location that meets demands for commuting to work. With decentralized workplaces, different jurisdictions become more or less attractive, and that makes parents' choices much more complicated than simply choosing a school.

Finally, for a variety of reasons, the public schools in adjacent jurisdictions may not look too different from one another. Central state restrictions; the limited viewpoints of school personnel in terms of curricula, pedagogy, and effective administration; and other things could lead schools to be quite similar in approach, curricula, and goals. The contraction of choices of different school districts when subsumed by the other choice aspects of residential location thus puts natural limits on how widespread any version of school choice such as Tiebout's might be. Few locales across the nation provide the optimum conditions for balancing the various interests of families in a way that allows genuine choice of schools to be effectively achieved.

Enter Milton Friedman. In his 1955 essay, Friedman provided a more compelling approach to securing the interests of parents in their children's schooling. Friedman acknowledged that government may want to intervene in education for a variety of legitimate reasons, but he argued that none of the potential reasons, including ensuring a minimal level of education for the population or enabling the children of the poor to attend school, requires government to actually run the schools. Friedman proposed that, although some sort of government financial mechanisms may be desirable, there was no reason why governments should be involved in the operation of schools.

Friedman thus compellingly proposed that the best means of balancing legitimate state interests and the natural interests of families would be to provide vouchers to parents. The vouchers would transfer funding to the government or nongovernment school that parents chose for their children to attend. Thus, within the context of the other aspects of locational decisions, parents could search for the optimum place for their residence on the basis of commuting, housing prices, and the range of services available in the jurisdiction. They could then use their school voucher to shop for the best school without having to make the other sacrifices possibly called for in Tiebout's scenario of school choice.

The Challenge of Implementation

The brilliance of the voucher idea has yet to be met with much policy success in the United States. A few cracks have developed in the resistance to vouchers, but nothing that looks like a general movement toward widespread implementation. It is useful to consider why this idea has not caught hold more quickly.

Perhaps the most obvious factor is the rise of teachers' unions. When school choice was originally introduced, teachers' unions were not pervasive. Their subsequent rise and increase in power, however, have forever changed the ability to introduce any radical new policy in schools. A fundamental precept and implication of competition in schools, namely, that the job security of some current personnel would be threatened, is anathema to unionized educators. Thus, any hint of even experimenting with school choice has been vigorously attacked by the unions. Their efforts to resist change, including powerful media campaigns to prevent citizen referenda on vouchers from being adopted, have been very effective.

Despite the significant braking effect of the unions on choice-based school reform, there remain grounds for hope. To set the scene for optimism, it is necessary to review the current state of experimentation with vouchers and other vehicles of choice.

Experience with Vouchers

Recent experiences with school choice include the introduction of a limited voucher program in Milwaukee, the introduction of a more broadly accessible program in Cleveland, the U.S. Supreme Court's affirmation of such policies, and the introduction of a variety of private voucher programs. These experiences have been discussed and analyzed in a variety of different places.[4] Although different authors and commentators have interpreted the data differently, my summary is fairly straightforward.

First, it is important to recognize that, whatever conclusions we might draw from these programs, none of them looks like a general test of a universal voucher program such as that proposed by Friedman. They rely (at least until recently) on schools in existence before the vouchers were introduced. Thus, they give little indication of any supply response that might be seen if there were a more far-reaching, universal voucher program that was sure to be available for some time into the future.

Second, in almost all situations the expenditure in the voucher schools is noticeably less than that in the competing public schools. That differential implies that present voucher programs are constrained tests of Friedman's voucher idea. On the one hand, if they survive with fewer resources, they demonstrate that competition can improve efficiency. On the other hand, limited resources may severely reduce the number of schools willing to enter the market and may dampen seriously the innovation that is seen.

Third, parents tend to be happier with the nongovernment schools they have chosen through the voucher programs than with the corresponding public schools.[5] In other words, even given the restrictions noted above, there is a group of parents that highly values the alternative schools.

Finally, the achievement of students receiving vouchers appears to be as high as or higher than that of students in comparable public schools. Allowing for possible differences in student bodies, those students opting out of government schools through a voucher program on average score better than those who apply for but do not receive vouchers—although this is not consistent across subgroups, across outcome measures, or across length of voucher program operation.

Despite the initial positive indicators observed in even limited experiences with vouchers, the current political situation is nonetheless easily summarized: there is as yet no strong political support for vouchers, and, while some states looked poised to try experiments, it seems unlikely that extensive new efforts will come to fruition.

Experience with Other Forms of Choice

One of the significant changes in the educational climate since the publication of Friedman's voucher proposal in 1955 has been the introduction of the principle of choice in schooling in other ways. Although universal vouchers are the purest form of choice, and the one obviously preferred by Friedman, innovation in choice has occurred.

Homeschooling

To begin with, there has been a considerable surge in homeschooling. A significant number of parents have simply withdrawn their children from the regular public schools and taken personal responsibility for their education. Some estimates put the number of homeschoolers at between 1.5 and 2 percent of all school children, although there is uncertainty even about the numbers involved.[6] Unfortunately, however, little is known about this in terms of movements of children in and out of homeschool environments or of their performance trends.

Intradistrict Open Enrollment

Citizen sentiment for expanded choice has generally increased over time, a fact not missed by opponents of more choice. Thus, one reaction to expanding calls for vouchers and more choice has been some people's mantra that they are for choice but it should be restricted to public school choice. That position has been particularly popular among politicians who want to protect the existing public schools from any competitive pressures yet still seem open to more fundamental reforms of schools.

A particularly popular version of public school choice involves an open-enrollment plan, under which, for example, students could apply to go to a different school in their district rather than the one to which they are originally assigned. In a more expansive version, no initial assignment is made at all, and students apply to an ordered set of district schools. A common version of this has been the use of magnet schools that offer a specialized focus such as college preparatory or the arts. Forms of open-enrollment plans were the response of a number of districts in southern states to the desegregation orders flowing from *Brown v. Board of Education*. In general, simple open-enrollment plans were not found to satisfy the court requirements for desegregation of districts, but magnet schools (with racial balance restrictions) became a reasonably common policy approach.[7] In 2001–02, 3 percent of all students attended magnet schools.[8]

It is fair to say that these public school choice plans do not even bear a pale resemblance to the ideas of choice included in voucher plans. First, the flow of students is heavily controlled. For example, the first caveat is always "if there is space at the school," but the desirable public schools virtually never have space. Second, large urban school systems where there is a natural range of options frequently face other restrictions, such as racial balance concerns, that severely constrain the outcomes that are permitted. Third, and most important, these plans seldom have much effect on incentives in the schools. The competitive model of vouchers envisions that schools that are unable to attract students will improve or shut down. That threat provides an incentive to people in the schools to perform well or to potentially lose their jobs. In a district with open enrollment, personnel in undersubscribed schools generally still have employment rights and simply move to another school with more students, diminishing the effect of competitive incentives.

Interdistrict Open Enrollment

Another variant of open-enrollment plans permits students in a city to attend any public school in the state. Conceptually, this could offer some competitive incentives. If a district lost sufficient students through out-migration, it could be left with less funding and could be forced to reduce its workforce. Again, however, the reality does not bring to bear many of the potentially positive effects of competition. In the first instance, voluntary interdistrict enrollment typically requires the approval of the boards of the schools a student is exiting and entering, meaning that the parents can face significant hurdles in making choices. The "if there is space at the school" clause generally stops all but some token movement. In addition, because of complicated formulas for school funding that mix federal, state, and local dollars, the funding following the choice student is typically less than the full funding for a student in the receiving district, meaning that any district accepting students is asking its residents to subsidize the education of students whose families reside and thus pay school taxes outside the district. The funding of transfers is also complicated by the common practice of basing current-year funding on prior-year enrollment or attendance figures, or both.

Charter Schools

The rise of charter schools has introduced an element of choice in schooling that promises to better mimic a genuine voucher program. Because they are creatures of the separate states and operate in different ways according to state rules, there is no common model of a charter school. The essential features are that they are public schools that are allowed to operate to varying degrees outside the normal public school administrative structures. To the extent that they survive through their ability to attract sufficient numbers of students, they are schools of choice. They differ widely, however, in the rules for their establishment, in the regulations that apply to them, in the financing that goes with the students, and in a host of other potentially important dimensions.[9] Some states, for example, impose a variety of requirements about teacher certification, curriculum, acceptance of special education students, and the like—advertised as "leveling the playing field"—in order to ensure that charter schools do not offer any true innovation and competition. Other states, however, remove a substantial amount of regulation and truly solicit innovation and competition.[10]

Despite the regulatory diversity surrounding them, charter schools can nonetheless offer true competition to the traditional government schools, because they can draw students away from poorly performing schools. Employment rights typically do not transfer between charters and existing school districts so there is potentially pressure on school personnel to attract students. Moreover, we see that charters are truly susceptible to the necessary downside of competition in that a substantial number of attempted charters do not succeed in the marketplace.[11]

Since the nation's first charter school legislation was enacted into law in Minnesota in 1991, some 41 states and the U.S. Congress, on behalf of the District of Columbia, have enacted legislation that provides for charter schools, although some had yet to open any schools by 2004. In the nation as a whole, charter schools increased from a handful in 1991 to more than 3,000 schools serving an estimated 700,000 students, or approximately 1.5 percent of the public school population, in 2004.[12]

In some places, charters have become quite significant. For example, in the 2001–02 school year, 9.2 percent of students in the District of Columbia, 6.7 percent of students in Arizona, 3.8 percent of students in Michigan, and 3.7 percent of students in California attended charter schools.[13]

What do we know about the performance of charter schools? Analysis has actually been very limited. To begin with, any school of choice—from the classic Catholic schools to charters and other schools that may emerge under a broad-scale voucher program— necessarily has a self-selected population. Thus, inferring the impact of the school, as distinct from the characteristics of the students who are attracted, is always difficult. In addition, because charter schools are largely new, most are still going through a start-up phase. The results observed during this phase may not be indicative of what they will look like in the steady state.

The situation is also complicated by the politics of charter schools. The teachers' unions, as part of their resistance to competition, gained national publicity for their simple comparison of scores of students in charter schools with those of students in regular public schools.[14] More serious work, however, has concentrated on adjusting for the special populations that choose charter schools.

My own work provides some preliminary estimates of the performance of charters in Texas.[15] Texas has a significant number of charter schools (although the legislature has capped the total number). Because Texas has tested students for a decade, it is possible to trace the students who enter and leave charter schools. The simplest research design that deals with the selection problems is a comparison of the average learning growth of individual students when in the regular public schools with their performance in the charters. In this way, charter students become their own control group.

Three things come out of this in terms of quality indicators. First, on average, charter schools perform very similarly to the traditional public schools. But, second, start-up problems are real, and new charters do not perform as well as more established charters. More established charters (those more than two years old) on average outperform the traditional public schools of Texas. Third, there is a significant distribution of performance across both traditional government schools and charter schools. The good are good, and the bad are truly bad.

Those findings are consistent with much of the other recent work on charter school performance, although there are some remaining uncertainties. The average North Carolina charter appears less effective than the average traditional public school,[16] whereas the average Florida charter is on a par with the traditional government schools after a start-up phase of two to four years.[17] On the other hand, relying on comparisons between charter applicants in Chicago who were randomly accepted or randomly denied admission, Caroline Hoxby and Jonah Rockoff conclude that the city's charter schools significantly outperformed their regular school counterparts.[18]

One other aspect of charter schools deserves mention. Schools selected on the basis of family choice, such as charter schools, have potential advantages attributable to allowing students to find schools that meet their own interests and needs. But another important aspect of competitive markets is enforcing a discipline on the other participants—in this case the traditional government schools. Is there any evidence that the traditional government schools respond to the pressures of competition? Even though it is still very early in the development of charters, Hoxby introduces preliminary evidence that there are competitive improvements.[19]

Our Texas study also provides information on the potential effects of competition. If we look at the behavior of parents, we find that they are significantly more likely to withdraw their children from a poorly performing charter school than from a charter that performs well. That finding is particularly important because parents are not typically given information on the comparative performance of their charter school. The behavior of parents shows, however, that they are good consumers and that they can use the performance data that are available to infer the quality of the school. An early and continual criticism of the voucher idea is that parents are not good consumers, an assertion belied by the data that emerge from observing the choices of charter school parents.[20]

It is useful to note that parents make similar judgments about the traditional government schools, but they are much less likely to exit such schools, given bad performance. The reason is obvious: it is generally much more costly to change government schools, given that a change of residence is usually required. Further, the ability to exit a given government school is not shared equally by all parents. Middle- and upper-income parents have the resources to select among alternative districts, which almost surely explains their generally greater satisfaction with the public schools.[21]

In the end, while charter schools are beginning to provide us some insights into the effects of broader options and choices in schooling, definitive assessment of the promise of charter schools awaits both the general maturation of more charter schools and the investigation of their performance in different settings.

Some Conclusions

The remarkable thing about our current discussions of choice is that much was predicted and anticipated by Milton Friedman when he wrote about these things a half century ago. First, he noted that parents indeed take a keen interest in the schools their children attend—and that shows up in the continued demand for expanding forms of choice. Second, although many people questioned the ability of parents to make good choices, the evidence available from even limited introductions of parental choice in the forms of homeschooling, open enrollment, and charter schools suggests that consumers are good decisionmakers even in these complicated markets.

What Friedman failed to appreciate fully was the resistance to choice. The potent political force of the teachers' unions with their vested interests has been successful in stopping much of the movement toward expanded choice. Nevertheless, there are reasons for optimism. High on the list is the growing recognition that American schools are extraordinarily expensive but not very effective.[22] That fact has been driven home by recent attempts to introduce accountability into schools, a move that has provided much more direct information to parents about the state of their schools.[23] One outgrowth of that is likely to be renewed energy for alternatives and the potential for even purer forms of school choice to be tested in the future.

Notes

1. National Center for Education Statistics, *Digest of Education Statistics, 2003* (Washington: U.S. Department of Education, 2004).

2. Ibid.

3. Charles M. Tiebout, "A Pure Theory of Local Expenditures," *Journal of Political Economy* 64 (October 1956): 416–24.

4. See generally Cecilia Elena Rouse, "Private School Vouchers and Student Achievement: An Evaluation of the Milwaukee Parental Choice Program," *Quarterly*

Journal of Economics 113 (May 1998): 553–602; and William G. Howell and Paul E. Peterson, *The Education Gap: Vouchers and Urban Schools* (Washington: Brookings Institution Press, 2002).

5. See John F. Witte Jr., *The Market Approach to Education* (Princeton, NJ: Princeton University Press, 1999); Howell and Peterson; and Paul E. Peterson, "The Theory and Practice of School Choice," Paper presented at a conference on the Legacy of Milton and Rose Friedman's Free to Choose: Economic Liberalism at the Turn of the Twenty-First Century, Dallas, TX, October 22–23, 2003.

6. Robin R. Henke, Phillip Kaufman, Stephen P. Broughman, and Kathryn Chandler, *Issues Related to Estimating the Home-Schooled Population in the United States with National Household Survey Data* (Washington: National Center for Education Statistics, September 2000).

7. See David J. Armor, *Forced Justice: School Desegregation and the Law* (New York: Oxford University Press, 1995).

8. See Lee McGraw Hoffman, *Overview of Public Elementary and Secondary Schools: School Year 2001–02* (Washington: National Center for Education Statistics, May 2003).

9. See Chester E. Finn Jr., Bruno V. Manno, and Gregg Vanourek, *Charter Schools in Action* (Princeton, NJ: Princeton University Press, 2000).

10. See Center for Education Reform, *Charter School Laws across the States: Ranking Score Card and Legislative Profiles* (Washington: Center for Education Reform, January 2003).

11. See Center for Education Reform, *Charter School Closures: The Opportunity for Accountability* (Washington: Center for Education Reform, 2002).

12. Current data on charter schools are fragmentary and must be pieced together from various private sources. See U.S. Charter Schools, http://www.uscharterschools.org; and Center for Education Reform, http://www.edreform.org.

13. See Hoffman.

14. See F. Howard Nelson, Bella Rosenberg, and Nancy Van Meter, *Charter School Achievement on the 2003 National Assessment of Educational Progress* (Washington: American Federation of Teachers, August 2004).

15. Eric A. Hanushek and Margaret E. Raymond, "Does School Accountability Lead to Improved Student Performance?" *Journal of Policy Analysis and Management* 24, no. 2 (Spring 2005).

16. See Robert Bifulco and Helen F. Ladd, "The Impacts of Charter Schools on Student Achievement: Evidence from North Carolina," Duke University, Terry Sanford Institute of Public Policy, SAN04-01, August 2004.

17. See Tim R. Sass, "Charter Schools and Student Achievement in Florida," Paper presented at American Economic Association annual meetings, Philadelphia, 2005.

18. See Caroline Minter Hoxby and Jonah E. Rockoff, "The Impact of Charter Schools on Student Achievement" (unpublished mimeo, November 2004). It is important to note that many of these assessments of charter schools are also biased against charter schools to the extent that the objectives of such schools may not simply be developing the basic math and reading skills that are used in the analysis. Little attention has been paid to evaluating how well charter schools achieve their own uniquely chosen specialized purposes.

19. See Caroline Minter Hoxby, "School Choice and School Productivity (or Could School Choice Be a Tide That Lifts All Boats?)" in *The Economics of School Choice*, ed. Caroline Minter Hoxby (Chicago: University of Chicago Press, 2003).

20. See Eric A. Hanushek et al., "Charter School Quality and Parental Decision Making with School Choice," National Bureau of Economic Research, March 2005.

21. See Terry M. Moe, *Schools, Vouchers, and the American Public* (Washington: Brookings Institution Press, 2001).

22. See Eric A. Hanushek, "The Failure of Input-Based Schooling Policies," *Economic Journal* 113, no. 485 (February 2003): F64–F98.

23. See Hanushek and Raymond.

7. Free-Market Strategy and Tactics in K–12 Education

Myron Lieberman

The task set for contributors to this book was to assess whether Milton Friedman's ideas on school reform have merit for the 21st century. My guess is that the Friedmans are bored with reading how right they are, so perhaps they will appreciate the effort if not the substance of my critical treatment here of the strategic prospects and needed tactics for advancing free-market school reform.

Over 50 years ago, Milton Friedman wrote one of the most interesting and insightful articles on the union movement that I have ever read. In that article, Friedman argued that the economic impact of the unions was greatly exaggerated and that he was not convinced that anti-union measures were required to remedy whatever abuses were found to exist. His analysis of unions was based on their impact as monopolists, and he did not rule out the possibility that action might have to be taken in the future to limit their monopolistic tendencies.

The article was completely devoted to private-sector unions and stands out for its prescience. Friedman was convinced that economic factors that the unions could not counteract would lead to the decline of unions, and that is what has happened in the private sector. Union membership in the private sector declined from 36 percent of the labor force in 1956 to 8 percent in 2004. Obviously, Friedman's views on the strategy and tactics to be adopted with respect to public-sector unions merit respectful consideration. In recent years, Friedman has opined that the teachers' unions are the major obstacle to improvement of our K–12 educational system, and I concur. We part company mainly on what to do about it.

I am inclined to believe that demographic and economic factors may weaken the power of teachers' unions to obstruct essential changes, but we cannot sit around waiting for that possibility to materialize 15 or 20 years from now. The National Education Association and the American Federation of Teachers have already launched a full-court press to achieve voluntary early childhood education for all paid for by government. The idea already has many supporters, such as the Committee for Economic Development. That is reason enough to review our strategies and tactics critically, and my analysis here is intended to be a contribution to that important task.

Whether Friedman's ideas on education reform continue to hold merit depends on the particular ideas selected for discussion. This implies that one or more of his ideas on school reform may not have merit for the 21st century, and I propose to discuss one such possibility, or cluster of possibilities: Friedman's strategy and tactics for achieving a free market in education. To my knowledge, the Friedmans have never comprehensively articulated a strategy and tactics, but they are presumably reflected in the Friedmans' statements from time to time on school choice issues and the policies followed by the Friedman Foundation. The policy discernible through these statements and actions is to bless every expansion of school choice, without any reservation or mention of its noncompetitive or anti-competitive features, and without pointing out that the outcomes under such school choice plans cannot reasonably be attributed to a free market in education and may even be antithetical to it. My point is not that the Friedmans or any supporters of a free market in education should necessarily have opposed such plans, but that minimally, they should have been more vocal in making it clear that school choice plans that prohibited parents from paying more than the voucher amount from personal funds, that required lotteries when schools could not accept all voucher-bearing students, that excluded for-profit schools from participating in voucher plans, and that did not provide any potential benefits of scale were not free-market school choice plans. Nothing in these comments implies that support should go or have gone only to school choice plans that have no impediments to a free market or should go only to ideal school choice plans. Undoubtedly, the mistakes in strategy and tactics, if such they be, are due partly to the Friedmans' good-faith effort to work as closely as possible with others in the school choice movement. Certainly, Milton's oft-asserted caveat against allowing the ideal to be the enemy of the good is a sentiment that all can share.

Nevertheless, clarification of "school choice" is essential. According to the National Working Commission on School Choice in K–12 Education, school choice "is any arrangement that gives parents options among schools. The question of whether 'choice' is a good thing has no single answer. Since the response depends on how choice is designed, the answer can vary from one design to another."[1]

Let us accept both the definition and the implication drawn by the National Commission—whether school choice is a good thing depends on the features of the plan in question. There is usually little point to controversies over "school choice" per se; what makes sense, or might make sense, is controversy over specific school choice plans. Otherwise, most controversy over school choice is like controversy over whether drugs are good for sick people, without any regard to the illness; the symptoms; or the dosage, frequency, and counterindications of the drugs.

The Basics of Free-Market School Choice

To ensure definitional agreement, let us start with Friedman's 1962 proposal that jump-started the contemporary school choice movement. Friedman's rationale for school choice was for a specific version of it—a free-market plan. Writing in 1955 and 1962, he relied on a wealth of evidence from thousands of industries worldwide that showed that competitive market systems produce and distribute goods and services of higher quality at lower costs than government does. Friedman did not see any plausible reason why the outcome would be any different in the provision of educational services.

Friedman regarded school choice primarily as a freedom issue: the freedom of parents to have children educated as the parents wish. This was an important freedom that should not be abridged in the absence of a strong reason for doing so. Friedman was also impressed by studies showing a very high literacy rate in England before the advent of compulsory education financed by government.[2] The gist of Friedman's argument was that private, for-profit operation of schools would raise the quality and lower the costs of schooling, that is, would have the same outcomes as it has in competitive industries generally. As a monopoly, public education by itself would not achieve the lower costs and higher quality that characterize competitive industries.

83

As an economist, Friedman was well aware that certain conditions must prevail in order to have meaningful competition in education markets. Ideally, those conditions include the following:

- Ease of entry. Providers should not be kept out of the market to protect other providers.
- No control of the market by any particular provider(s) or consumer(s).
- Reasonably good information about offers and acceptances.
- Freedom of providers to sell to anyone and freedom of consumers to buy from anyone at prices mutually agreed upon.

Those conditions are matters of degree. There are very few markets in which those conditions are present without some qualification or deviation from the ideal. In fact, Joseph Schumpeter has argued that perfect competition is impossible and would be undesirable if it were possible.[3] In any case, "imperfect competition" characterizes the overwhelming majority of competitive goods and services. A "free market" in education does not mean a system free of all regulations and limitations on competition.

Several changes since the structure of public education was established more than a century ago have strengthened the case for a market system of education:

- Transportation has improved tremendously, weakening the importance of proximity to the schools, especially at the middle and secondary levels.
- Most parents are much better educated than parents were a century ago. This suggests that most are better able to evaluate educational services than were parents, often first-generation immigrants, when public education was being established.
- As government grows, the competition for tax funding becomes more and more intense. The demands for benefits and services for seniors are especially threatening to public education since the number of seniors is expected to increase dramatically while the birthrate, except for immigrant families, is expected to decline, thereby weakening political support for government-funded K–12 education.
- Increases in the urban population have made competition much more feasible than it was when our nation was largely a rural,

agricultural society. Furthermore, the development of information technology has provided more alternatives for rural areas.
● American society has become much more diverse. This has led
to increased conflict over education, and hence to correspondingly higher social and economic costs of such conflict at the
local, state, and national levels.[4] Praise for diversity cannot con-
ceal the fact that it has led to a great deal of social conflict over
several aspects of government-run schooling.[5]

It is hardly possible to overemphasize the importance of the requisite conditions for a market system. To the extent that they are
absent, there is no free-market school choice plan.

The importance of understanding the essence of a free education
market cannot be overstated. Analysts and pundits frequently cite
the outcomes of voucher plans that lack the critical characteristics
cited above as evidence that free markets cannot be effective in
education. Jeffrey R. Henig's book, *Rethinking School Choice*, is explicitly devoted to demonstrating the limitations of the "market metaphor" in education. Referring to a voucher proposal by John E.
Chubb and Terry M. Moe, Henig identifies it with the Friedman
model, asserting that

> the Chubb and Moe proposal is designed to accommodate
> a few redistributory and regulatory provisions that Friedman
> did not mention, but that are not directly contrary to his
> basic design.[6]

This conflation of the Chubb and Moe proposal with a Friedman-
style plan is egregiously mistaken. Moe was one of the small group
of proponents of vouchers who declined to support Proposition 174,
a 1993 California voucher initiative endorsed by Friedman. Moe's
later book on vouchers explicitly asserts that vouchers did not make
any headway until their supporters concluded that the free-market
voucher was wrong in principle and ineffective politically.[7] Furthermore, the Chubb and Moe book advocated several restrictions on
vouchers that Friedman strongly opposed. For example, Chubb and
Moe advocated a prohibition against parental add-ons to the
voucher amount.[8]

There is, however, much stronger evidence that Henig did not
understand the essential features of a market system, and because
his criticisms of such a system have received widespread attention,

85

his failure to understand it merits attention. In his book, Henig asserted that "in an initiative that comes closer than any other to approximating the voucher model that Friedman envisaged, Wisconsin in 1990 began a program to allow low-income Milwaukee residents to attend private schools with tuition assistance from the government."[9]

In fact, however, the Milwaukee voucher plan did not even remotely resemble a free-market plan. The main features of the Milwaukee plan when Henig wrote his commentary were the following:

- Participation in the voucher plan was restricted to 1 percent of the enrollment in the Milwaukee public schools. Accordingly, maximum potential participation in 1990–91 was 936 pupils in grades K–12.
- Pupils who participated had to be from families whose incomes did not exceed 175 percent of the poverty level.
- Voucher students could not exceed 49 percent of any school's population.
- For-profit schools and schools affiliated with religious denominations were ineligible to participate.
- Participating schools were required to accept all voucher-bearing students as long as space was available.
- If the number of voucher students exceeded the number of spaces available, applicants had to be selected by random lottery.
- The Milwaukee school district was required to provide transportation, as it would for public school students.
- The amount of the voucher was set at 53 percent of the average amount spent per pupil in the Milwaukee public schools in 1990–91 (approximately $2,500).
- Participating schools did not receive additional funds for learning-disabled or emotionally disturbed pupils, as did the public schools.
- Schools that redeemed vouchers could not charge students more than the amount of the voucher.

Henig's analysis contains egregious mistakes concerning market systems and illustrates the inaccuracies and poor scholarship that characterize most criticism of free-market voucher plans.[10] Sad to say, the tendency to characterize every existing voucher program as a free-market plan prevails even among writers who might be expected to know better. According to an editorial in the *Wall Street Journal*, "Milwaukee became the first major city to institute a real voucher program—and the public schools responded by improving."[11] Despite common assertions to the contrary, the Milwaukee program did not and does not bear close resemblance to "Mr. Friedman's idea," whatever its paternity may be.

Similar problems appeared around the D.C. voucher program. Prior to enactment of the D.C. voucher bill, a federal official with major responsibilities for the Bush administration's school choice programs urged enactment of the D.C. voucher bill "to settle once and for all whether school choice works."[12] The implication that the viability of a competitive education industry would rest on the outcomes of a congressional voucher plan with several anti-competitive features illustrates two points. First, it gives (unflattering) insight into the sophistication of the Bush administration on voucher and competition issues. Second, it illustrates the price being paid for the failure to emphasize that the outcomes of noncompetitive school choice plans cannot be attributed to plans that foster significant competition. Unfortunately, as long as the media and most of the professional literature do not draw any distinctions between school choice plans, the acceptability of free-market plans is dependent on the outcomes of plans that are the antithesis of free-market positions on school choice.[13]

Equalitarian and Free-Market Divergence

Although Friedman's voucher proposals have received some attention from economists, they have been more ignored than rebutted in the literature on education. The failure to examine Friedman's ideas on their own terms stems in part from the countervailing interest of the education establishment and its elevation of equity issues over issues of freedom or innovation and improvement, or both. The biases of the education establishment today may be related to the upheavals over school integration and the Great Society legislation of the 1960s; it is difficult to see how Friedman's free-market voucher proposal could have upstaged the controversies over racial discrimination and segregation in education, the launch of several federal programs expected to remedy the effects of racial discrimination (such as Head Start), and teacher unionization; any one of these developments would have left little energy, political or intellectual, to cope with the idea of a competitive education industry. Furthermore, some southern states and school districts adopted school choice plans as a way to avoid racial integration, and these actions led to black opposition to school choice that continues to be cited almost half a century later as a reason to oppose it.

As it became clear in the 1970s and early 1980s that reformist measures were not leading to significant improvement, educational vouchers emerged again as an idea to be reckoned with, but with rationales that differed from Friedman's. School choice was couched as a moral issue, a freedom of religion issue, an equity issue, and, in recent years, as a civil rights issue. The supporters of school choice continued to mention the benefits of competition, but that was pro forma; by 1990 "competition" was merely a rhetorical add-on to other arguments for school choice. While proponents of school choice mentioned the benefits of competition, they supported school choice plans like the one in Milwaukee that could not possibly bring about significant market competition in K–12 education.

The Milwaukee plan was not conceived as a step toward a broader free market in education; on the contrary, its minority leaders, such as Polly Williams and Howard Fuller, explicitly stated that they would oppose expansion of the plan to middle-class students.[14] Moe praised the Milwaukee plan:

> Milwaukee was the dawning of a new era. . . . Since Milwaukee, the voucher movement has attracted a very different following: more equalitarian in outlook, less impressed with free markets, less concerned with religion. Many conservatives in its ranks continue to see vouchers in universalistic and market-oriented terms. But to many of the newer supporters, vouchers are not just about choice, competition and performance incentives. Nor are they necessarily for all children. They are about bringing equal opportunity to the children in greatest need.[15]

Moe's comment illustrates why I have characterized the division in the school choice ranks as one between "equalitarians" and "free marketeers." That division goes back to the late 1960s and 1970s. In 1978 John E. Coons and Stephen D. Sugarman published *Education by Choice.* In the preface to the 1996 edition, they observe that in the 1970s they were "puzzled that many champions of school choice pictured the market as its own justification" and concluded that the "curious idolatry of the market has provided enemies of choice with what is still their favorite target."[16]

The divisions between equalitarians and free marketeers came to a head in 1993 with the voucher initiative in California. The initiative ultimately went on the ballot as Proposition 174, but it had been preceded by basic disagreement between Friedman, who supported a free-market version, and Coons, Sugarman, and Moe, who supported critical anti-competitive provisions, such as a ban on family payments for tuition in addition to the voucher amount. In the most widely read education book of the 1990s, Chubb and Moe stated: "While it is important to give parents and students as much flexibility as possible, we think it is unwise to allow them to supplement their scholarship amounts with personal funds. Such 'add-ons' threaten to produce too many disparities and inequalities within the public system, and many citizens would regard them as unfair and burdensome."[17] In contrast, Friedman pointed out the absurdity of allowing parents to spend for liquor, tobacco, and other harmful products while denying them the right to spend more on the education of their children.

Why restricting parental freedom to pay more for education from their own resources is "unfair and burdensome" is not clear, nor is it clear why the parties sought to promote their voucher plans in California, the state with the strongest opposition to any educational voucher plan. In any event, Friedman's views on Proposition 174 prevailed; it was a free-market plan that did not include the restrictions to ensure equity supported by Moe, Coons, and Sugarman. Consequently, the equalitarians declined to support Proposition 174, which was defeated by a seven-to-three margin in November 1993.[18]

Since the failure of Proposition 174, equalitarians have held the upper hand, and their point of view is now widespread and entrenched in the media and at Harvard, Stanford, Princeton, the Manhattan Institute, the Heritage Foundation, the Brookings Institution, and the Fordham Foundation. Even the Hoover Institution's Koret Task Force on Education includes more equalitarians than supporters of a free market in education. The equalitarians suck up philanthropic and government resources and media attention in efforts to promote their school choice plans. This entrenchment was epitomized recently when the Fordham Foundation awarded Moe its annual (2005) $25,000 prize for scholarship. In announcing the prize, Chester E. Finn Jr., president of the foundation and chairman of the Hoover Institution's Koret Task Force on Education, referred to Moe as the "godfather" of the school choice movement. The implications of that characterization should not be ignored.[19]

Moe has provided the most detailed rationale for the equalitarian position. Its main features are as follows:

- Means-tested vouchers are the most effective way to provide equality of educational opportunity, especially for low-income minorities in our large urban school districts.
- The American people have consistently rejected a free-market version of vouchers by wide margins. A majority will not accept the kind of unregulated vouchers being promoted by the free marketeers.
- Americans like the public school system and will reject changes that weaken it.
- Government regulation is essential to ensure accountability, fairness, and equality.
- Although vouchers may eventually be available to all children, at this time, the American people will accept only vouchers targeted to needy children and incremental change.
- Two-thirds of the American people have never heard about vouchers, according to their responses in polls.[20]

Moe's analysis was part of his study of public opinion on vouchers. The study was primarily devoted to analyzing polls on vouchers to ascertain the basic features of public opinion on the subject. As Moe interpreted it, the American people have repeatedly and decisively rejected the free-market position on vouchers. Moe interpreted the defeat of voucher initiatives in California and in Michigan in 2000 as additional confirmation that only means-tested voucher legislation would be acceptable to the American people, and then only if it were not seen as a stepping stone to a free-market version.[21] His view is that, as liberals recognize that more and more conservatives support means-tested vouchers on their merits, not as a strategic move to bring about a market system of education, support for vouchers will continue to grow. That point of view flatly contradicts the idea held by many advocates of a free market in education that "school choice" plans, whatever their content, will eventually lead to a competitive educational system. In fact, Moe has felt vindicated by the political decline of the free-market rationale for vouchers.[22]

Nevertheless, the equalitarian strategy was not effective in the 2000 elections, in which the Gore/Lieberman ticket, strongly backed by teachers' unions, received a record high 90-plus percent of the black vote, a critical constituency that must be won over for any eventual success of school choice. Moe himself has emphasized that the teachers' unions are the most powerful political interest group in the United States, a consideration that suggests minimal progress even for equalitarian school choice plans for many years to come.[23]

Competition as a Means to Equity

In arguing that the American people will not accept a free market in education, Moe adopts a restrictive view of "free markets" and paints an unduly optimistic picture of the benefits of regulation. His position on both the free market and the effects of regulation further reflects his fundamental opposition to a competitive educational system.[24]

At the center of the discussion about the prospects for school choice is a persistent failure to understand the dynamics of competition. In opposing competition, its critics often argue that it leads to negative practices. For-profit health maintenance organizations cut services to the patients who need expensive medical services. Competition to attract outstanding high school athletes leads college coaches to offer illegal inducements to enroll at their institutions or to alter high school transcripts. Athletic competition leads institutions of higher education to establish easy-to-pass courses and lower their admission requirements. The criticism is that the supporters of competition ignore its negative effects, sometimes referred to as "the race to the bottom," in their argument that competition will force schools to improve or go out of business.[25]

Although there *are* negative effects of competition, as there are of any system, they are not the reason for the opposition to competition. I base this conclusion on the absurdity of the other reasons cited for opposing a market system. For example, consider the following question and answer at a forum on school choice: "What are the features of K–12 education that render producer competition inappropriate in education?" The answer by Gerald Bracey, one of the nation's leading critics of competition in education, was that education is a service, not a product. That answer is patently absurd; competition is alive and well in hundreds of service industries, such as dry cleaning and air travel. Yet after decades of educational and political conflict over competition in education, this is the intellectual level of the debate—with only more obfuscation in sight.

To be candid, the proponents of "school choice" are as much responsible for this situation as are the opponents. By enthusiastically embracing every school choice plan while claiming that school choice fosters competition, they have fostered the confusion about and neglect of the conditions required for significant competition to materialize.

Let me cite one additional aspect of the Milwaukee voucher plan that underscores the urgent need to clarify the essentials of a competitive educational system. In recent years a number of voucher analysts, some of whom approve and some of whom disapprove of the Milwaukee program, have investigated the extent to which the program led to changes in the Milwaukee Public Schools. Researchers favorable to school choice found that the voucher program led to a more responsive MPS; for example, public schools had open houses to familiarize parents with school programs. Reassured by this, the supporters of school choice could hardly wait to rush into print to spread the news that school choice results in competition. Unfortunately, no one points out that research and development funded from profits are the source of most of the improvement and lower costs of our goods and services. I do not wish to denigrate improvements that materialize in the absence of "R&D" funded from profits, but the complete analytical neglect of the major source of improvement in free markets, and its total absence in Milwaukee-type programs, indicates that the supporters of school choice are often as unsophisticated about the free enterprise system as are their opponents.

There is an urgent need at present for advocates of free-market school choice to clarify the essentials of a competitive educational system and its potential to bring about more equitable access to desirable schools. Free-market philosophy such as that articulated by Friedman argues that the poor have benefited the most from free markets because they could not afford the goods and services prior to the reductions in costs and improvements in quality that resulted from competition. There is no serious challenge to the fact that this has been the outcome in widely different industries in countries all around the world. Consequently, the question that should be asked is this: Why wouldn't the same outcome materialize in education if public schools, denominational and other nonprofit private schools, and for-profit schools were required to compete for students who received vouchers and were free to accept any additional amounts agreed upon by the students' families and the schools? Despite thousands of articles and books on school choice, this question is not explicitly answered or even raised by most critics of the free-market approach to vouchers.

With different views about how educational equity is best attained, supporters of school choice understandably differ on the extent of government regulation they will accept. Libertarian free-market supporters want to restrict government regulation of private schools to health and safety regulations applicable to schools generally, preferring as little regulation as possible, but it is inaccurate to portray them as insistent on the complete absence of regulation or on limiting regulation to health and safety issues. Their main concern is that state education bureaucracies hostile to vouchers will try to regulate them out of existence. That concern underlies much of their opposition to regulation, and their experience provides ample justification for their concern.[26]

Equalitarians want to include a variety of measures intended to bring about equity in every school choice plan. Those measures include the prohibition of add-ons, the requirement that private schools that admit voucher-bearing students reserve a certain percentage of admissions for children from poor families, and the use of lotteries when there are more applicants than vacancies. These and other measures favored by equalitarians drastically weaken competition. Thus, to say that "school choice" offers options may mean much or little, depending on the quality and cost of the options.

Unfortunately, the equalitarians have exaggerated the benefits of the school choice plans that have been adopted. The exaggerations may be the outcome of a good-faith belief in the success of the plans, but all too often the supporting evidence is not evaluated as critically as the opposing evidence. In any event, the fact that school choice leads to "competition" can be true but highly misleading because the actual level of competition may be marginal. The kind of competition that matters is the kind that is characterized by research and development to identify more effective services or to lower the cost of production by a substantial margin. That is not the kind of competition that has emerged or will emerge from equalitarian school choice plans.

If and when vouchers are available under the kind of competition that matters, there is no obvious reason why they will not lead to more effective educational services at much lower costs. Therefore, it is essential to avoid restrictions that would virtually forestall competition and the research and development that lead to industry-wide improvement. This is the single most important issue of regulation under school choice.

Most citizens accept inequalities that are essential to raise the welfare of everyone. This does not mean that school choice programs cannot or should not make any concessions to an equalitarian point of view. Such concessions may be desirable in their own right or necessary for political purposes, but concessions that eviscerate competition should be avoided.

In school choice legislation, there will have to be tradeoffs, and the tradeoffs will have to be made in a specific context. For this reason, it is difficult to say what deviations from a free market would be acceptable. Free marketeers do not oppose school choice proposals that merely enable some students to attend different public schools, *but such proposals cannot generate significant market competition.* The damage is done when the equalitarians claim that they are supporters of competition and claim also that their proposals will bring the benefits of competition. Helping children from poor families attend a different and presumably better school is not necessarily fostering competition; the claim that it does is naïve and jeopardizes support for school choice plans that really would foster competition.

In the equalitarian view, competition is an incremental process; equalitarians do not expect any fundamental change in the process except over a long period of incremental changes.[27] However, this is not the way leading economists think about basic changes. In his classic study of capitalism, Schumpeter pointed out that the most important advances occur by a process of "creative destruction" when an entire industry is revolutionized: from horse-drawn carriages to gasoline-fueled cars, ship to airplane travel, frozen food instead of canned food, and so on. In his words:

> The first thing to go is the traditional conception of the *modus operandi* of competition. Economists are at long last emerging from the stage in which price competition was all they saw. As soon as quality competition and sales effort are admitted into the sacred precincts of theory, the price variable is ousted from its dominant position. However, it is still competition within a rigid pattern of invariant conditions, methods of production and forms of industrial organization in particular, that practically monopolizes attention. But in capitalist reality as distinguished from its textbook picture, it is not that kind of competition which counts but the competition from the new commodity, the new technology, the new source of supply, the new type of organization (the largest-scale unit of control for instance)—competition which commands a decisive cost or quality advantage and which strikes not at the margins of the profits and the outputs of the existing firms but at their foundations and their very lives.[28]

Realistically, there is no chance of such a development under equalitarian plans. The investment in educational research and development emerging from means-tested school choice plans, if any, has been miniscule. Such plans are not a threat to the established order; in fact, they may strengthen it. What is likely to happen—in fact, what is happening—is that means-tested vouchers are propping up the system they are supposed to replace.

Albert O. Hirschmann's analysis of monopolies explains the reasons why Milwaukee-type voucher plans strengthen the status quo. Hirschmann distinguished two kinds of monopolies. One kind, "profit-making monopolies," fights aggressively "to prevent any deviation or exception." The other kind, labeled "lazy monopolies," seeks to avoid conflict with parties who are likely to challenge the monopoly unless they get what they want.[29] The lazy monopolies tolerate, and may even foster, alternatives that will satisfy the potential dissidents. Thus, the public school establishment, which is a lazy monopoly, does not challenge parents' right to send their children to private schools at their own expense. If every child were required to attend public schools, the resulting conflicts might jeopardize the lazy monopoly.

Similar considerations apply to means-tested vouchers. They provide alternatives that satisfy urban minority leaders who would
otherwise participate in broader attacks on public schools. A solution
that provides the activists with an acceptable alternative without
jeopardizing the status quo meets the needs of the lazy monopoly;
one of the coalition constituencies, having gotten a solution that
satisfies it, is no longer supportive of the broader aims of the coalition. As pointed out previously, several black leaders supportive of
vouchers are strongly opposed to vouchers for the middle class.
Thus we come to an unpleasant but unavoidable conclusion: the
equalitarians, for all their good intentions, are pursuing a course of
action that does not and will not lead to basic changes in the status
quo. The reasons can be summarized as follows:

- The emphasis on equalitarianism has strengthened the errone-
  ous assumption that no major changes are needed if we can
  improve the educational achievement of disadvantaged
  minorities.
- The equalitarian voucher plans have not provided and cannot
  provide the benefits of competition; however, by claiming that
  their voucher plans foster competition, the equalitarians are
  jeopardizing the acceptability of voucher plans that would foster it.
- Equalitarian plans attract and satisfy activists who are essential
  to enact competitive school choice plans.
- Whatever innovations of general applicability may emerge from
  equalitarian school choice programs will face an extremely difficult time getting accepted in middle- and upper-class school
  districts. Such districts are not likely to accept the idea that
  innovations in economically disadvantaged areas have any relevance to their situation.
- Means-tested vouchers are not leading to investment in R&D
  or innovations that improve the efficacy of public education.
- Parent satisfaction with schools of choice is an extremely weak
  reason to support equalitarian school choice plans, especially
  if school choice was supported initially as the way to raise
  educational achievement. Furthermore, most parents, including
  most minority parents, are satisfied with their public schools
  (though in many cases this is arguably due to lack of objective

evidence on their children's actual performance compared with the performance of students in other nations or with their likely performance under a free-market system).

- The equalitarian school choice plans are not likely to foster educational innovations that would be useful in many schools. This is more likely to happen under free-market plans because for-profit schools will seek larger, that is, nonethnic and nondenominational, markets.

As was previously pointed out, most improvement in goods and services results from research and development funded from profits. No profits, no research and development. No research and development, no improvement in services. The situation is further exacerbated by the equalitarian insistence on means-tested vouchers, which results in a small market at the low end of the economic base. In the real world, this is a prescription for continued stagnation. The vast majority of goods and services has improved because the affluent paid for the initial innovation; then, over time, the cost was brought down by research and development. Airplanes, air travel, computers, automobiles, medical technology, telephones, refrigerators—the list is endless, but the pattern has been basically the same. Essentially, the equalitarians are trying to achieve equity by policies that ignore economic realities, including the benefits of market competition. Unfortunately, noble purpose is no guarantee of policy effectiveness.

There is perhaps one model we might be able to learn from. Food stamps are a voucher program that neither weakens the benefits of a competitive food distribution system nor restricts the recipients from adding to the amount of the voucher. Similarly, we should foster equality of educational opportunity, but not by eviscerating the benefits of a free market in education.

Some Conclusions about Strategies and Tactics

In conclusion, let me suggest a few actions that would be helpful in efforts to achieve a competitive education industry. My first suggestion is about as thrilling as "Let's form a committee," but the preceding discussion explains its importance. The absence of a coalition damages the political prospects of school choice; however, an effective coalition is unlikely to emerge unless the advocates of school choice become more united in their political efforts. Therefore,

I suggest that the supporters of the free-market position publish a statement that points out the requisite conditions for a competitive education industry or a school choice plan that is worthy of support on this basis, or both. The statement should be distributed widely enough to give every interested party, especially education reporters and editors, a convenient opportunity to learn how and why the free-market position differs from other versions of school choice. The statement should be sent to the *New York Times*, the *Wall Street Journal*, the *Washington Post*, *Education Week*, and to all of the leading education and public policy journals. It should also be disseminated to every think tank and philanthropic foundation active on education issues. And it should appear in Friedman Foundation publications. The statement should assert that the signers are unlikely to support school choice legislation that excludes for-profit schools unless, as a minimum, the sponsors agree publicly to support expansion of the program to for-profit schools. Of course, the signatories are free to oppose noncompetitive school choice plans for other reasons.

Second, there is an urgent need for media education on the differences between the free-market position and all others. Year after year, liberal foundations have sponsored programs for the media through the Hechinger Institute and the Education Writers Association, with predictable results. Because media personnel employed by public school organizations are allowed to be voting members of EWA, and conservative philanthropy does not contribute to EWA or to the Hechinger Institute, it is difficult to overcome EWA's tilt toward the public school establishment.

Third, free marketeers should stop writing and talking as if the issue were whether we should replace all public schools with for-profit or private schools. It is necessary only that for-profit schools have a reasonable opportunity to demonstrate their potential. What happens after that can be left to the citizenry that has to resolve the issues. My surmise is that a 10 or perhaps a 5 percent market share would be more than enough to resolve the remaining policy issues relating to a market system.

Fourth, in my opinion, free marketeers should not support, let alone lionize, school choice leaders with the equalitarian point of view. Bear in mind that equalitarian plans create interest groups and leaders who oppose free-market plans. I would not require school choice leaders to be enthusiastic supporters of a free market, but I would require their support as a quid pro quo for ours, even though a free-market version may not be possible at the time our support is requested.

Fifth, I suggest that we stop using the phrase "failing public schools." Many proponents of public education are deeply concerned about the enormous power of the teachers' unions. Free marketeers and equalitarians lose their support by the constant references to "failing public schools." As I go back to my high school reunions, it is obvious that none of my classmates feels that he or she attended a "failing school," and that characterization would have been very off-putting.

Many of us remember the conservative reaction to the Coleman Report, a study of the impact of racial segregation on academic achievement. The U.S. Department of Education, which sponsored the study, anticipated that it would show that racial segregation had a major negative impact on educational achievement. When the study showed instead that family background had a much larger impact, conservatives were delighted because it supported their views on the importance of family factors. According to conservatives today, however, the low levels of academic achievement are due solely to "failing public schools." Supposedly, all children would become proficient if it were not for our "failing public schools."

From a free-market point of view, whether public schools are "successful" or "failing" is irrelevant. The Model T was a great success, but it was part of a system in which producers had to improve their products in order to survive. Up to this time, the supporters of a free market in education have strengthened the fallacious view that all would be well if we could just reduce the achievement gap.

Sixth, I suggest that we avoid the fashionable reference to school choice as a "civil right." To my knowledge, none of the proponents of this view, including President Bush, has told us what is meant by "civil right." Is medical care for children a civil right? From birth or starting at school age? Does this civil right ever end? If so, at what age or event? If a state decided to go out of the K–12 education business, whose civil rights would be violated? I do not recommend unilateral rhetorical disarmament, but we should avoid language that could come back to haunt us. The future of the free-market position does not depend on the use of rhetoric that is counter to the free-market position.

Finally, I reiterate that the free-market version of school choice should be publicized as soon as possible. The No Child Left Behind Act will not bring about significant improvement in K–12 education despite equalitarian efforts to prop it up. The inherent inadequacy of the act will probably be widely recognized before the end of President Bush's second term. At that point in time, there will be renewed interest in "school choice," but what version of it will be the focus of discussion and of action? If free marketeers hope to see a free-market version anywhere in the United States, they cannot wait until the day of reckoning for NCLB to educate policymakers about their differences with the equalitarians. If supporters of a free market in education have not challenged the equalitarian version of school choice until then, discerning where they can be allies and where they must not compromise, they will not be able to avoid paying the price of guilt by association. There is a better way.

Notes

1. Paul T. Hill, *School Choice: Doing It the Right Way Makes a Difference, A Report from the National Working Commission on Choice in K–12 Education* (Washington: Brookings Institution Press, 2002), p. 11.

2. See generally E. G. West, *Education and the State,* 3d ed. (1965; Indianapolis: Liberty Press, 1994).

3. Joesph A. Schumpeter, *Capitalism, Socialism and Democracy* (New York: Harper & Row, 1976), pp. 77–78, 103–5.

4. Mark Harrison, *Education Matters: Government, Markets and New Zealand Schools* (Wellington, New Zealand: Education Forum, 2004), pp. 364–69.

5. Increased diversity has not led to an increase in conflict within the private education sector.

6. Jeffrey R. Henig, *Rethinking School Choice: Limits of the Market Metaphor* (Princeton, NJ: Princeton University Press, 1995). Henig's reference is to John E. Chubb and Terry M. Moe, *Politics, Markets, and America's Schools* (Washington: Brookings Institution Press, 1990). Henig's book was initially published in 1994; the 1995 edition includes a 20-page afterword.

7. See generally Terry M. Moe, *Schools, Vouchers, and the American Public* (Washington: Brookings Institution Press, 2001).

8. Chubb and Moe, p. 220.

9. Henig, p. 110.

10. My criticism in this paragraph takes into account the following books and too many articles to list: Chubb and Moe; Henig; Moe, *Schools, Vouchers, and the American Public;* Joseph P. Viteritti, *Choosing Equality* (Washington: Brookings Institution Press, 1999); Edward B. Fiske and Helen F. Ladd, *When Schools Compete* (Washington: Brookings Institution Press, 2000); John Witte, *The Market Approach to Education: An Analysis of America's First Voucher Program* (Princeton, NJ: Princeton University Press, 2000); Bryan P. Gill et al., *Rhetoric versus Reality* (Santa Monica, CA: RAND, 2001); and Richard D. Kahlenberg, ed., *Public School Choice vs. Private School Vouchers* (New York:

Century, 2003). There are huge qualitative differences between these books, and it should be emphasized that my comment is intended to apply only to their treatment of free-market school choice plans. Of the seven books listed, three are pro-choice, three are anti-choice, and one asserts that there is as yet no clear-cut case for or against vouchers.

11. "An Idea Has Consequences," *Wall Street Journal*, May 5, 2004, p. A20.

12. Nina S. Rees, quoted in Caroline Hendrie, "Researchers See Opportunity in DC Vouchers," *Education Week*, February 4, 2004, pp. 1, 14. The full quote is "'This study could once and for all answer the key question of whether the act of choosing to send your child to a private school is one that leads to higher student achievement,' said Nina S. Rees, a deputy undersecretary in the U.S. Department of Education, whose office of innovation and improvement will oversee the voucher program."

13. John Merrifield, *The School Choice Wars* (Lanham, MD: Scarecrow, 2001), pp. 20–43.

14. Howard Fuller and Polly Williams, orally to the author, circa 2002.

15. Moe, *Schools, Vouchers, and the American Public*, p. 35.

16. John R. Coons and Stephen D. Sugarman, *Education by Choice: The Case for Family Control* (Berkeley: University of California Press, 1978; Troy, NY: Educator's International Press, 1996), pp. ix–x.

17. Chubb and Moe, p. 220.

18. Moe, *Schools, Vouchers, and the American Public*, pp. 359–65.

19. Parenthetically, I'm surprised that a more intensive effort has not been made to bring free marketeers and equalitarians together. Knowing most of the leaders involved, one might think this was a lost cause, but my collective bargaining experience suggests otherwise. Collective bargaining frequently begins with divisions that appear to be insurmountable but are eventually overcome under the necessity of reaching agreement. Psychologically, that necessity is not felt yet in the school choice camp.

20. See generally Moe, *Schools, Vouchers, and the American Public*.

21. Ibid., pp. 376–77.

22. Ibid., p. 22.

23. Terry M. Moe, "No Teacher Left Behind," *Wall Street Journal*, January, 13, 2005, p. A12.

24. Moe, *Schools, Vouchers, and the American Public*, p. 23.

25. See generally Robert Kuttner, *Everything for Sale: The Virtues and Limits of Markets* (Chicago: University of Chicago Press, 1996).

26. For example, in Wisconsin the state superintendent of public instruction vigorously opposed the voucher legislation and tried to establish several regulations that would have undermined the legislation after it was enacted.

27. Moe, *Schools, Vouchers, and the American Public*, pp. 344–97.

28. Schumpeter, p. 84.

29. Albert O. Hirschmann, *Exit, Voice and Loyalty* (Cambridge, MA: Harvard University Press, 1970).

8. A Critique of Pure Friedman: An Empirical Reassessment of "The Role of Government in Education"

Andrew Coulson

When *Capitalism and Freedom* was reprinted in 1982, Milton Friedman remarked that advocacy of limited government and individual liberty had been outside the philosophical mainstream of the 1950s. "Those of us who were deeply concerned about the danger to freedom and prosperity from the growth of government, from the triumph of welfare-state and Keynesian ideas," he wrote, "were a small beleaguered minority regarded as eccentrics by the great majority of our fellow intellectuals."

Most distantly removed from the mainstream was Friedman's assertion that public education was best pursued through the private sector. Consider that just 20 years before Friedman penned "The Role of Government in Education," the National Education Association had complained that "the competitive, laissez-faire system" was crippling "our attempts to create the necessary new social procedures and accompanying institutions" and declared that the time had come for "the frank acceptance of the collective economy."[1] Not only did early 20th-century education philosophers oppose privatizing their own industry, they advocated nationalizing many others.

Who was right, the intellectual majority or the "eccentric" champion of market education? Thanks to a half century of accumulated research, it is now possible to address that question empirically. This essay seeks to do just that, assessing how well Friedman's work of pure reason stands up to the international and historical evidence.[2]

"The Role of Government in Education" is a philosophical exploration. From a set of fundamental axioms about human nature and human societies, Friedman deduces that a school voucher program would be preferable to the government monopolies that dominated the educational landscape in 1955, and continue to dominate it today.

His discussion has two main parts. First, he asks whether, and on what grounds, government can rightly intervene in the field of education and, second, having concluded that such intervention can be justified, he asks what form it should take. This essay reviews the empirical evidence bearing on these matters. In addition to his main arguments, Friedman also theorizes about the relative cost and effectiveness of government versus market provision of education. There is insufficient space in the present work to evaluate those theories in detail, but they are briefly mentioned in the conclusion.

Justifications for Government Intervention

Can government intervention in general education be justified and, if so, on what grounds? Friedman discusses two principal arguments for such intervention: neighborhood effects (a.k.a., externalities) and paternalism. The empirical case for each is described below.

Neighborhood Effects

In Friedman's usage, a neighborhood effect exists whenever the actions of one person confer benefits (or impose costs) on other people and it is not possible to charge (or compensate) those other people through strictly voluntary exchanges (because the people affected cannot all be identified or because the magnitude of the effects cannot be objectively measured, or both). Friedman stipulates that democracies cannot survive unless their citizens have at least some minimal level of general education, and so there are significant positive neighborhood effects associated with acquiring that education. Friedman therefore concluded in his 1955 essay that neighborhood effects justify some sort of government intervention to ensure adequate general education.

That reasoning relies on, but leaves unstated, a basic assumption about externalities: that services with significant positive externalities will not be consumed in "sufficient" quantity if the benefits to society are greater than the benefits to the individual consumer. Sufficiency in this context is defined as the level of consumption required to produce some desired social outcome. An example would be automobile liability insurance. The benefit to a driver of being insured against damage he might cause to other people's property is not as great as the benefit to society of requiring all drivers to have such insurance. It is because of that discrepancy that automobile liability insurance is so often mandatory. So by concluding that some form of government intervention was warranted in education because of its neighborhood effects,[3] Friedman implicitly assumed that in the absence of such intervention parents would consume too little education to sustain democracy.

To gauge the validity of that assumption on empirical grounds, we can review the historical evidence on school consumption prior to significant state involvement. If the assumption is valid, then U.S. school enrollment should have risen steadily and substantially between 1852 and 1918, when compulsory education laws were introduced around the country and the provision of government schooling greatly expanded and became increasingly centralized at the state level. Prior to that period, the consumption of education was entirely voluntary in the United States, and "government" schooling was a comparatively modest, locally operated endeavor.

The historical record does not reflect the pattern just described. Between 1850 and 1900, the enrollment rate of white 5- to 19-year-olds declined by 2.6 percentage points. It then rose by 12 percentage points over the next two decades.[4] Nonwhite enrollment stagnated below 2 percent from 1850 to 1860, rose to 31.1 percent in 1900, jumped to 45 percent by 1910, and hit 53 percent in 1920. Those enrollment trends are not hard to explain. Prior to the Civil War, it was illegal for African-American children to be educated across the South. When slavery was abolished and those laws repealed, there was a surge in the enrollment of black children. The reason that white enrollment stagnated during the second half of the 19th century is that elementary schooling was already virtually universal among the free population by that time, and there was simply no room for it to increase.[5]

High school consumption was miniscule,[6] but a formal high school education was not necessary for most careers before the 20th century (or, de facto, for the preservation of democracy during that period). High school attendance did not become the norm until well into the 20th century, when technological and commercial advances caused it to be perceived as a necessity, and when a rising standard of living, combined with urbanization, meant that families had less and less need for the labor of their teenaged children.

Insufficient consumption of education for the preservation of democracy thus does not appear to have been a serious problem under the voluntary educational arrangements that predated modern state-run school systems and mandatory attendance laws.[7] The only shift in government policy that clearly had a significant positive effect on enrollment was the elimination of laws forbidding African Americans to attend school.

It could nevertheless be argued that government intervention in education, in the form of preexisting semipublic schools, predated the rise of mandatory attendance laws and state-run public school systems. The bureaucratic state-run public school systems familiar to modern readers were an innovation of the late 19th and early 20th centuries. Prior to that time, government involvement in precollegiate education was uneven and generally limited to local "district schools," essentially cooperatives overseen by the families they served. District schools were usually free for only the poorest families in a community. Others contributed directly for their own children's education, so the total value of the "public" subsidization of education was only a fraction of the total spending by district schools.

District schools were only one option in a diverse marketplace that encompassed a range of private-sector options. Those options included small, very inexpensive schools operated out of the teachers' own homes (sometimes referred to as "dame" schools), more formal academies, charity schools funded by churches and philanthropic organizations, and schools run by guilds and mutual aid societies. Detailed analyses of 19th-century British data indicate that most children continued to be educated in fully parent-funded private schools decades after a government-subsidized alternative became available.[8] It was only when the subsidy grew to represent a substantial share of total per pupil costs that it began to erode the preexisting high levels of parent-funded private-sector enrollment.

Consumption of subsidized semipublic schooling was greater in the early-19th-century United States than in the United Kingdom, but education was nevertheless voluntary during that period, and most parents had to make some direct financial sacrifice to pay at least a portion of their own children's educational costs. District schools did make it easier for some families to consume education than would have been the case in a purely private education market, but the magnitude of their impact on consumption could not have been especially large, and an expansion of existing privately funded alternatives might have made up much of the difference had district schools not existed (we know from E. G. West's analysis, for instance, that increases in public school funding were contemporaneous with decreases in private school consumption).[9]

What conclusion can we draw from this discussion? Even if we grant that general education has positive neighborhood effects, there is little empirical support for the assumption that such education is insufficiently consumed in the absence of government intervention or heavy government subsidization.[10] Whether or not government becomes actively involved in schooling, citizens seem to voluntarily consume enough education for the perpetuation of democracy. Thus the argument that government involvement in general education is justified on the grounds of democracy-sustaining neighborhood effects is not strongly supported by the evidence. Friedman later reached the same conclusion himself in the 1980 book *Free to Choose*, coauthored with his wife Rose, and maintains that position to this day.[11]

Social Stability

The previous discussion of neighborhood effects focused on the minimum level of general academic education necessary to execute the duties of citizenship, such as basic literacy and numeracy and familiarity with the nation's laws and government. That education is concerned with knowledge and skills. Friedman also acknowledges a related neighborhood effects hypothesis that has been put forward by others: "that it might . . . be impossible to provide the common core of values deemed requisite for social stability" without government operation of schools. Tied up in this values hypothesis is the notion that democratic control over schooling strengthens communities and promotes harmonious social relations, whereas unfettered parental choice in a private education market would have a Balkanizing effect on society.

Friedman acknowledges that this notion has been persuasive but cautions that "it is by no means clear that it is valid or that denationalizing [i.e., privatizing] schooling would have the effects suggested."[12] He also adds that fully tax-funded state-run school systems conflict with the American principle of individual freedom because they make it harder to consume nongovernment schooling (some of the income that parents might wish to spend on private schooling is forcibly taken as taxes and used to pay for the government schools, creating a financial incentive to opt for government schooling instead of possibly preferred private schooling).

Are Friedman's skepticism and concern justified, or is it truly necessary for children to be indoctrinated by the state? Is educational diversity intrinsically Balkanizing as the values hypothesis implies? The most reliable and empirical way of answering those questions is to conduct what are called "natural experiments." In a conventional scientific experiment, researchers randomly assign subjects to "treatment" and "control" groups and carefully measure differences in the outcome of interest. In some fields, such as epidemiology and anthropology, formal randomized trials are either morally unacceptable or practically impossible. Epidemiologists cannot unleash plagues for the purpose of studying alternative treatments, nor can anthropologists replay history to see how North America might have turned out if never visited by Amerigo Vespucci and Cristoforo Colombo. Education policy analysts are in a similar fix. What they can do, however, is to marshal the evidence that is available and conduct natural experiments, such as

- observing how a given type of school system has performed across differing cultural and economic settings throughout history,
- observing how different types of school systems have performed under comparable cultural and economic conditions, and
- observing how social and educational outcomes have changed (or haven't changed) when societies have moved from one type of school system to another.

I adopted this approach in studying a wide range of school systems from ancient Greece to modern America in my book *Market Education: The Unknown History* and found no evidence to support the hypothesis that government schooling is necessary for social harmony or stability. Indeed, I found the opposite. Government coercion, not diversity, has historically been the chief source of education-related social discord. Education systems that have facilitated free parental choice have seldom induced Balkanization. Instead, they have tended to diffuse tensions by permitting different groups within societies to pass along their unique religious or cultural heritage unmolested. It is state-run schooling that has most often set neighbor against neighbor in battles for control of the official curriculum.

Upon reflection, those findings should not be surprising. Since all taxpayers are obliged to pay for government schools, all want those schools to reflect their own views and to reject views they oppose. In pluralistic societies, that is impossible. The result of government-funded schooling is a relentless series of "school wars" in which different ideological constituencies compete to impose their own orthodoxy on the state-funded organs of education. As I wrote in *Market Education*:

> Prior to the [U.S.] government's involvement in education, there were nondenominational schools, Quaker schools and Lutheran schools, fundamentalist schools and more liberal Protestant schools, classical schools and technical schools, in accordance with the preferences of local communities. Some had homogeneous enrollments, others drew students from across ethnic and religious lines. In areas where schools of different sects coexisted, they and their patrons seldom came into conflict, since they did not try to foist their views on one another. They lived and let live in what were comparatively stable, though increasingly diverse, communities. It was only after the state began creating uniform institutions for all children that these families were thrown into conflict. Within public schools, many parents were faced with an unpleasant choice: accept that objectionable ideas would be forced on their children, or force their own ideas on everyone else's children by taking control of the system.[13]

Sectarian Protestantism was the norm in public schools from the 19th through the early 20th century. The Protestant Bible was required reading for public school children. Catholic and other students who failed to comply were sometimes beaten, and when such beatings were legally challenged, they were generally upheld by the courts. When Catholics fought for and won the right to use their own Bible in their neighborhood public schools in place of the Protestant one, their success precipitated the Philadelphia Bible Riots of 1844,[14] in which 13 people lost their lives and St. Augustine's church was burned to the ground. The rise of public schools also led to the official denigration of immigrant values, beliefs, and lifestyles in

LIBERTY & LEARNING

classes and textbooks, and to the famous "monkey" trial in which Tennessee public school teacher John Scopes was prosecuted for, and found guilty of, teaching the theory of evolution in a public school. The evolution vs. creation battle of course rages on in public schools to this very day,[15] having sprouted several offshoots such as "scientific creationism" and "intelligent design" theory.

The conflict-riddled history of U.S. public schooling is not unique. From the medieval Islamic empire, to post-Reformation Germany, to the Netherlands of the early 20th century, state-run schooling has consistently precipitated conflicts over the content of the official curriculum. In the Netherlands, much of that conflict was successfully defused by the adoption of a nationwide parental choice program that includes private schools. For those interested readers, further cases are chronicled in *Market Education*.

If the notion that government schooling breeds social harmony is thus at odds with reality, what of the related belief that democratically run schools are uniquely capable of imbuing children with the values essential to the survival of democracy? In discussing this belief, the authors of a 2001 RAND Corporation book aptly note that "[t]here have not been many formal theoretical defenses of the democratic value of public education; its defenders have relied largely on rhetorical recapitulations and refinements of traditional common school notions, as well as lamentations about the insidious effects of individualistic market-oriented philosophies."[16]

Such notions and lamentations are contradicted by the available evidence. David Campbell offers this assessment based on his own recent research:

> A survey of students currently enrolled in private schools suggests that when compared to public school students, they are more likely to engage in community service, develop civic skills in school, express confidence in being able to use those skills, exhibit greater political knowledge, and express a greater degree of political tolerance. Data from a randomized experiment of applicants to a national school voucher program confirm these results for political tolerance, but not for political knowledge. Based on these findings, it would appear that when compared to their publicly educated peers, students in private schools generally perform better on multiple indicators of their civic education. More specifically, there is no reason to think that school vouchers would inhibit the

110

civic development of those who use them to attend private schools. On the contrary, students who switch from public to private schools show an increased level of political tolerance, what theorists stress as a fundamental component of civic education.[17]

Campbell's findings are consistent with the earlier work of Paul Hill for the Brookings Institution,[18] as well as the work of Richard G. Niemi and Christopher Chapman for the federal Department of Education's National Center for Education Statistics (published, it should be noted, under the pro-state-schooling Clinton administration).[19]

It also seems likely that meaningful racial and economic integration would improve under a free-market education system with financial assistance to ensure universal access. First, because private schools have been shown to more effectively promote meaningful voluntary integration among students than public schools[20] and, second, because the catchment-area-based student assignment rules prevailing in most public school districts exacerbate residential economic segregation (the wealthy exercise public school choice by purchasing homes in expensive neighborhoods that are not accessible to lower-income families).[21]

The cherished notion of American public schools as a benign melting pot is thus belied by the institution's actual history and contemporary effects. According to the available empirical evidence, public schooling has turned out to be inferior to market schooling in the promotion of democracy-sustaining values. What's more, the unavoidable element of coercion integral to tax-funded government schooling has consistently been a source of social conflict across nations and across time. The evidence thus favors Friedman's view that there is no net positive neighborhood effect of government schooling from the standpoint of values education or social harmony.

Paternalistic Concerns

Though Friedman cites paternalistic concerns as his second key justification for some sort of government intervention in education, he does not explore this justification in detail. Here I review three possible concerns that present themselves: that parents might choose to provide their children with "insufficient" education, that they might choose the "wrong" sort of education, or that they simply might not have the financial resources to provide their children with as much education as they, and their fellow citizens, would like.

The first of those possibilities, that there might be a systematic pattern of parents deliberately withholding education from their children, is unsupported by the evidence. Throughout history, parents have in fact voluntarily made every effort to consume education in proportion to its value in the prevailing cultural, political, and economic setting. As already noted, elementary schooling was all but universal among the free population in early-19th-century America, even though it was entirely voluntary. Since there is no evidence that significant numbers of parents will deliberately withhold education from their children, this particular paternalistic concern justifies neither compulsory attendance laws nor the government operation of schools.

Consider that we do not have laws mandating what, how much, or when children must be fed, despite the fact that there are occasional documented cases of parents starving their children. We have child abuse laws to handle the aberrant cases rather than child feeding laws to mandate what everyone normally does. There is no obvious reason why education should be treated differently. Parents who deliberately and maliciously kept their children uneducated could be handled just as we currently handle those who deliberately and maliciously starve their children.

What about our second concern, the educational judgment of parents? There are really two questions here: will parents seek the "right" sort of education (meaning, in this context, the sort of education that the rest of the public wants them to seek), and will parents be able to correctly identify schools that actually deliver that sort of education if left to their own devices? If the answer to either question is no, then a paternalistic argument could be made for intervening in parents' education decisionmaking.

I addressed the first of those questions at length in *Market Education*. After sifting through decades of international public opinion data, I found that parents generally have the same sorts of educational aspirations and expectations for their own children that the public at large has for others' children. That is true when it comes to academics, career preparation, basic character and moral education, and the school environment (e.g., physical safety and health concerns). There are certainly areas of parental and public disagreement over such things as the proper role of religion in education,

112

but those tend not to be areas in which the public seeks to compel uniformity. Few citizens of free nations want to impose a particular faith on all students, for example. When it comes to the particular skills, knowledge, and values that the public *does* want to see taught to all children, parents have proven themselves to be effective proxies for the public's paternalistic wishes. They generally do the right thing without the need for compulsion.

That brings us to the second part of the question: are parents capable of obtaining the sort educational services that they and their fellow citizens want without some sort of intervention from the state? In other words, can parents tell a good school from a bad one? This question implicitly relies on the assumption that curriculum decisions imposed through the political process will necessarily be wise, or at least wiser than those made by parents. Otherwise, there would be no point in having the state intervene.

Remarkably, that assumption is seldom acknowledged, let alone defended, by the proponents of this paternalistic argument for government intervention. It can certainly be granted that parents vary in their ability to make wise educational choices, but there is no a priori reason to assume that politically imposed decisions are, on the whole, superior. That is a testable hypothesis that, when put to the test, is quickly found to be false.

After comparing parental and government education decisions in dozens of historical and contemporary settings, I have found no evidence of systematically greater wisdom on the part of governments (whether democratic or otherwise). On the contrary, the evidence suggests that parents generally make better decisions for their own children than elected or appointed officials make on their behalf.

Consider a few examples. Familiarity with the English language is of considerable economic value in the developing world, just as it is in wealthy nations. For that reason, it is highly prized by parents. And yet, in much of Africa and the Indian subcontinent, state-run schools tend to offer English language instruction relatively sparingly—sometimes not at all. In those regions, private venture schools almost invariably offer classes in English, with many schools operating in English across their entire curriculum.[22] The private sector responds to consumer demand for an undeniably valuable service, while the state sector is comparatively unresponsive, pushing a syllabus that is disconnected from contemporary needs. In the United

States, public schools adopted one pedagogical fad after another over the course of the 20th century, from the "word method" (a precursor of "whole-language"), to "life-adjustment education," to "open classrooms," and so on. Private schools proved less gullible, and also quicker to come to their senses when they realized they had made pedagogical mistakes. The difference in susceptibility to educational gimmickry between the two sectors can to a great extent be attributed to the fact that private schools are directly answerable to parents—who are keenly focused on educational outcomes.[23]

Across nations and across time, the services that families have demanded and received from private schools have generally been comparable to, if not of greater quality than, those offered in government-run schools. In a survey of the international research on the relative effectiveness of state-run versus private schools, I counted 20 findings showing superior academic achievement among private school students, 5 showing no statistically significant difference, and only 2 showing a public-sector advantage. All of the findings showing a private-sector advantage controlled for family and student characteristics known to be associated with achievement, whereas one of the two findings showing a public-sector advantage did not (it ignored the fact that the tested public schools were academically selective whereas the private schools were not). The other finding of a public-sector advantage applied only to two newly created private schools within the private-sector sample. The rest of the private schools in the sample outperformed their public-sector counterparts.[24]

Having dispatched the first two arguments for government intervention on paternalistic grounds, we are left with the third and last: that some parents cannot afford to purchase as much education for their children as they, and their fellow citizens, desire. The limited financial resources of low- and middle-income families are obviously not in dispute, so the question is, do taxpayers want children to have more than a few hundred or a few thousand dollars worth of education annually? The answer is clear: in free nation after free nation, per pupil government spending on education has increased steadily since it was introduced, and it now stands at very substantial levels—$10,000 per year in the United States. In total, taxpayers currently spend roughly $120,000 on each American child's K–12 public education—far more than many families could hope to spend on their own.

So, while there is no evidence that parents will deliberately under-consume education, or that they need government oversight in directing their children's education, it is clear that majorities (or at least pluralities) of voters have consistently and repeatedly given their approval to government education spending levels far in excess of what many parents could afford if left to their own devices. This suggests that paternalistic concerns, at least those based on shortages of household resources for education, may provide some basis for collective action in education.

What Sort of Action Is Justified?

Paternalistic concerns do thus appear to justify some sort of collective action by the public, but does collective action necessarily mean government action? Could the private sector meet this paternalistic concern through voluntary philanthropic arrangements?

That is a difficult question to answer empirically. Prior to the rise of state schooling in the United States and the United Kingdom, for instance, there were private philanthropic efforts to secure broad access to education—efforts that atrophied in direct response to the rise of tax-funded government schooling.[25] But those voluntary arrangements were neither as universal, nor as uniform, nor as responsive to families' demands as modern citizens would likely demand. Perhaps citizens could erect an effective and responsive system of universal tuition assistance on an entirely private, voluntary basis, but such a system would be unprecedented.

Since resolving this question empirically currently seems impossible (short of actually trying it out), I will assume for the sake of this discussion that the collective educational action mandated on paternalistic grounds will involve the state in at least some limited capacity. The question then becomes, what sort of government involvement is optimal? In other words, what is the best way of ensuring that all families can afford to consume sufficient schooling of sufficiently high quality? Practically speaking, this breaks down into three subquestions: Should the assistance be universal or means tested? Should it be uniform or provided on a sliding scale? Should it be accomplished through government vouchers or tax credits?

When those issues are broached in "The Role of Government in Education," Friedman states that "it would be highly desirable to

115

impose the costs [of education] directly on the parents," with "spe-cial subsidy provisions for needy families." This targeted, or means-tested, approach to allocating state funding, Friedman argued, "would reduce the likelihood that governments would also adminis-ter schools" and "would increase the likelihood that the subsidy component of school expenditures would decline as the need for such subsidies declined with increasing general levels of income." He cautioned that "[i]f, as now, the government pays for all or most schooling, a rise in income simply leads to a still larger circular flow of funds through the tax mechanism, and an expansion in the role of the government."[26]

What does the empirical evidence say about the relative merits of direct parental funding versus government funding? In the past few decades, many studies have been conducted comparing parent-funded private schools with both government-funded private schools and government-run schools.[27] The pattern emerging from this literature is that private schools paid for directly by parents tend to be more efficient, more academically effective, better physically maintained, and more responsive to parental curriculum demands than either of the other arrangements for funding and governance.[28] That pattern has been observed in widely varying settings. Some of the most persuasive findings have come from the developing world, such as Geeta Gandhi Kingdon's research showing the widespread consumption of private parent-funded schooling in India—school-ing that produces better results at a lower cost than its public-sector, or publicly funded private-sector, counterparts (the last of which so closely resemble state-run schools as to be indistinguishable from them, according to Kingdon).[29]

Another compelling example is an enormous World Bank study of government and nongovernment education in Indonesia, drawing on data from 68,000 schools. Researchers Estelle James, Elizabeth M. King, and Ace Suryadi found that the efficiency of both public and private schools was directly proportional to their share of local funding, and the local funding was made up principally of tuition and other fees paid by parents. In other words, the greater the share of a school's budget that comes directly from the parents it serves, the better that school runs.[30]

I have reached a similar conclusion in reviewing historical educa-tion systems, finding that schools funded directly by parents have

116

tended to be more responsive to their demands than those funded by third parties, whether the third party was an agency of government or a large philanthropic organization.[31]

In addition to considering school quality, efficiency, and responsiveness, it is important to assess the broader social impact of parent versus tax funding. As Friedman points out elsewhere, state intervention can produce negative externalities of its own that may offset its perceived advantages.[32] The modern and historical evidence does suggest that this is a serious concern with regard to the government funding of education. Whenever taxpayers have been compelled to fund educational services that violate their personal convictions (or when parents have been forced or pressured to consume government schooling), it has resulted in social tensions. Examples from American history have already been chronicled above, including the ongoing battle over the teaching of evolution versus biblical creationism. The fact that schooling funded through compulsory taxes has frequently resulted in social tensions is another reason to minimize the use of government funding and maximize the share of school costs that is borne directly by parents.

To sum up, Friedman appears to be correct in observing that direct parent funding is generally superior to government funding of private schools in terms of both individual school-level services and broader social effects. Several corollaries follow: (1) Means-tested subsidies are ultimately better than universal subsidies because they maximize direct parental funding and minimize government involvement. (2) Subsidies that vary in size on the basis of need are superior to uniform subsidies because they increase the direct financial responsibility of parents. (3) Tax credit programs are apt to be superior to government voucher programs in terms of both school-level and social effects because they rely solely on private funding, minimizing taxpayer compulsion and maximizing the direct financial responsibility of parents.

In later public writings, Friedman has reiterated his view that direct payment of tuition by parents is still the ideal, but he has advocated the use of universal government vouchers of uniform size as the best migration path to that goal.[33] I have written elsewhere on the relative merits of universal vouchers and education tax credits[34] and here will only quickly mention the positive argument for tax credits as a better way of meeting both the criteria set out by

Friedman and the corollaries I list above: tax credit programs are better equipped to simultaneously maximize direct financial responsibility of parents and ensure sufficiency of funding for universal access to the education marketplace.

Tax credit programs can be designed to serve both middle- and low-income families. Middle-income families can be given credits allowing them to keep more of their own money, and thus more readily afford nongovernment schooling. Low- and lower-middle-income families can be provided with private scholarships that are financed through tax-credit-eligible donations (taxpayers donate to a private scholarship fund and receive a credit in the amount of their donation, and the fund then disburses the money to families who need it). The financial assistance that the public deems desirable, and for which Milton Friedman finds logical support, can thus be provided without involving a single dollar of government funding.

Conclusion

The empirical evidence available to date largely supports Milton Friedman's conclusions that state-run schooling is unjustifiable in a free society and that education is best delivered through the private sector, supplemented by some financial assistance mechanism to ensure universal access.

Friedman's logical analysis has proven remarkably prophetic. Indeed, the foregoing discussion does not do justice to the full scope of his predictions. In addition to his main thesis, Friedman also makes a number of related conjectures about the quality and efficiency of public and private schooling that have been borne out by the evidence. He observes, for instance, that "[c]ompetitive enterprise is likely to be far more efficient in meeting consumer demand than nationalized enterprises."[35] Data on both domestic and international education strongly support that assertion.[36] Friedman notes that increases in public school spending are not likely to substantially improve the quality of education services. That has certainly been the U.S. and foreign experience of the past five decades.[37] Finally, Friedman cautioned that setting teachers' salaries according to a fixed scale, instead of tying them to performance and to market demand for particular skills, would undermine the ability of public schools to recruit and retain top talent. A recent econometric investigation of this question confirmed Friedman's analysis.

All of these predictions were offered at a time when most people, particularly most intellectuals, could not even imagine a world without state-run schools, let alone see its merits. In the 1982 introduction to his essay collection, *Capitalism and Freedom*, Friedman wrote that dramatic shifts in public policy are not generally precipitated by scholarly dissertations. The scholar's role, he suggested, is not to single-handedly bring about change but rather to "keep the lights on" during periods when mistaken ideologies dominate public policy and discourse. Few scholars have shone more brilliantly, over a longer span of time, than Milton Friedman.

Notes

1. John L. Childs, "A Preface to a New American Philosophy of Education," in *Social Change and Education, the 13th Yearbook of the Department of Superintendence of the National Education Association* (Washington: NEA, 1935), pp. 121–22.

2. Because of my limited familiarity with the research on higher education, I deal only with Friedman's analysis of general primary and secondary schooling.

3. As the following section explains, Friedman concludes that the *nature* of that justifiable intervention is largely limited to providing financial assistance.

4. This 12 percent rise among 5- to 19-year-olds may even overstate the actual enrollment gain from 1900 to 1920, since the enrollment data for 5- to 17-year-olds, a group closer to the normal school age-range of the time, of all races, rose by only 5 percent during the same period. See U.S. Bureau of the Census, *Historical Statistics of the United States: Colonial Times to 1970*, Bicentennial Edition (Washington: U.S. Government Printing Office, 1975), H 419, H 433–35, pp. 368–70.

5. Accurately interpreting the mid-19th-century U.S. enrollment data is difficult for a variety of reasons. First, the available population breakdowns by age are insufficiently precise. During the early to mid-1800s, most children attended school for six or seven years, roughly from the age of 6 or 7 to the age of 13, after which they worked on family farms or in family businesses, or were apprenticed to learn a different trade or business. Only a small minority went on to further studies. Even as late as 1871, the census reported only one high school student for every 100 elementary school students. See U.S. Bureau of the Census, H 422–44, p. 369. Unfortunately, historical population data for children are broken down into fixed five-year categories, beginning with ages 0–4, followed by 5–9, and so on. There is thus no direct correspondence between the available enrollment numbers and the actual school-aged population. Another complicating factor is that census workers in developing nations (a category into which the United States fell during the period in question) have been shown to significantly undercount enrollment in informal private educational arrangements such as schools operated out of teachers' own homes. For the 19th-century British evidence on this point, see Philip W. Gardner, *The Lost Elementary Schools of Victorian England: The People's Education* (London: Croom Helm, 1984), and for contemporary Indian data, see Geeta Gandhi Kingdon, "Private Schooling in India: Size, Nature, and Equity-Effects," *Economic and Political Weekly* 31, no. 51 (1996): 3306–14, http://www.econ.ox.ac.uk/Members/geeta.kingdon. PublishedPapers/privateschoolinginindia.pdf. Informal arrangements, including

homeschooling, were substantially more common in early-19th-century America than they are today, and so the published enrollment figures may be substantially biased downward. With these caveats in mind, we can obtain a very rough estimate of the enrollment rate in 1860 by taking the total elementary and secondary enrollment figure and dividing it by a fraction of the 5- to 14-year-old population. Using figures from the U.S. Bureau of the Census, we can compute that total enrollment was 2,639,919. The total population of 5- to 14-years-olds in 1860 was 3,881,567. Taking the average duration of formal schooling at between seven and eight years, we can very roughly estimate the school-aged population as between 2,717,097 and 3,105,254, which would yield an (elementary school) enrollment rate of somewhere between 87 and 99 percent. This gross nationwide enrollment rate estimate for 1860 is consistent with earlier figures from the New England states, where both the percentage of children being educated and the duration of their school careers were ahead of the rest of the nation. The Superintendent of Schools for New York City reported in 1836, for example, that "it is reasonable to believe, that in the common schools, private schools and academies, the number of children actually receiving instruction is equal to the whole number between five and sixteen years of age." Quoted in E. G. West, "The Political Economy of American Public School Legislation," in E. G. West, *Education and the State: A Study in Political Economy*, 3d ed. rev. (Indianapolis: Liberty Fund, 1994), p. 304.

6. In 1871, the earliest year for which a nationally representative enrollment breakdown is readily available, there were 100 elementary students for every secondary student. See U.S. Bureau of the Census, H 422–24, p. 369.

7. Further empirical support for this hypothesis comes from the difference in enrollment increases for 5- to 17-year-olds versus 5- to 19-year-olds (the only age ranges for which data are available). Though the latter group saw a 14 percentage point rise in enrollment (for all races) between 1900 and 1920, the former saw only a 5 point increase. But most early mandatory attendance laws applied only to children up to the ages of 14, 15, or 16, so they would not have applied to the older students who clearly account for much of the post-1900 increase in education consumption. This suggests that variations in the consumption of education between 1850 and 1920 were in large part the effect of changes in consumer demand (i.e., an increase in demand for general secondary, vocational, and higher schooling) rather than the result of government intervention.

8. See the discussion of these analyses in Andrew J. Coulson, *Market Education: The Unknown History* (New Brunswick, NJ: Transaction Books, 1999), pp. 88–89, 93–94.

9. West, p. 304. Further evidence that citizens will consume a "sufficient" quantity of education regardless of government intervention comes from modern India, where even the abjectly poor in urban slums, and to a lesser extent in rural villages, often pay for private fee-charging education even though free government-run schooling is generally available. They do so on the grounds that the government schooling is of insufficient quality and provides a less relevant curriculum. For excellent research on this topic, see James Tooley and Pauline Dixon, "Private Education Is Good for the Poor: A Study of Private Schools Serving the Poor in Low-Income Countries," Cato Institute white paper, December 7, 2005, http://www.cato.org/pub_display.php?pub-id + 5224. See also my summary of some of the relevant existing literature in Andrew J. Coulon, "Implementing Education for All: Moving from Goals to Action," Paper presented at the Fondazione Liberal's Second International

Education Conference, Milan, Italy, May 17, 2003, http://www.schoolchoices.org/roo/coulson_milan-(2003).pdf.

10. It is possible, however, that what was true of the United States and Great Britain in the 19th century, and what is true of India and other developing countries today, would not be true for modern welfare states. The reason is that the existence of private educational services that are financially within reach of even very poor families may depend on the absence of the welfare state. In nations with generous welfare benefits, ultra-low-cost private schooling is exceedingly rare, because there is little or no economic incentive for educators to operate schools at bargain-basement tuition rates when they might earn only slightly more from their efforts than they can receive via the welfare system. Both the historical and contemporary cases cited to demonstrate the sufficient consumption of education without government intervention come from nations that, during the periods at issue, had or have no significant welfare state. If government provision of education were eliminated today in the United States, it seems plausible that the ultra-low-cost options would be limited.

11. Milton Friedman and Rose Friedman, *Free to Choose* (New York: Harcourt Brace Jovanovich, 1990), pp. 162–63; and Milton Friedman, personal e-mail communication with the author, March 10, 2006, in which he wrote: "Whether government subsidy is justified for external effects of elementary and secondary education depends on an empirical question: what fraction of children would be schooled if there were no government subsidy? If that fraction is high, then there may be an external effect on the average but there is no marginal effect. It would make a negligible difference if 98 percent of children got schooled instead of 97 percent. However, it would make a major difference if 50 percent of children got schooled instead of 97 percent."

12. Milton Friedman, "The Role of Government in Education," in *Capitalism and Freedom* (Chicago: University of Chicago Press, 1982), p. 90.

13. Coulson, *Market Education*, p. 85.

14. Ibid., p. 82.

15. John Hanna, "Attorneys for, against Evolution Spar at Hearing," Associated Press, May 9, 2005, http://www.kansas.com/mld/kansas/news/state/11599482.htm.

16. Brian P. Gill, P. Michael Timpane, Karen E. Ross, and Dominic J. Brewer, *Rhetoric versus Reality: What We Know and What We Need to Know about Vouchers and Charter Schools* (Santa Monica, CA: RAND Corporation, 2001), chap. 7, http://www.rand.org/publications/MR/MR1118.

17. David E. Campbell, research report, University of Notre Dame, 2002, http://www.nd.edu/~amdemoc/Campbell_civiced.pdf.

18. Paul T. Hill, "What Is Public about Public Education?" research report, University of Washington and Brookings Institution, 2000, http://www.brook.edu/dybdocroot/GS/brown/PublicEd.PDF.

19. Richard G. Niemi and Christopher Chapman, "The Civic Development of 9th- through 12th-Grade Students in the United States: 1996," National Center for Education Statistics, statistical analysis report, 1998, http://nces.ed.gov/pubsearch/pubsinfo.asp?pubid=1999131.

20. Jay P. Greene and Nicole Mellow, "Integration Where It Counts," Paper presented at the annual meeting of the American Political Science Association, 1998, http://www.educationreview.homestead.com/Integration.html.

21. Thomas Nechyba, "School Finance, Spatial Income Segregation and the Nature of Communities," research report, Duke University and the National Bureau of

Economic Research, 2002, http://www.econ.duke.edu/~nechyba/segregation_revision.pdf.

22. Andrew J. Coulson, "How Markets Affect Quality: Testing a Theory of Market Education against the International Evidence," in *Educational Freedom in Urban America*, ed. David Salisbury and Casey Lartigue (Washington: Cato Institute, 2004), pp. 265–324.

23. Coulson, *Market Education*, p. 274.

24. Coulson, "How Markets Affect Quality."

25. West, p. 304.

26. Friedman, p. 87.

27. Coulson, "How Markets Affect Quality."

28. There are exceptions to this pattern, however. On an international test known as the Program on International Student Assessment, government-subsidized private schools were found to academically outperform privately funded private schools in student reading achievement. No controls were provided for school spending, however, and so the relative efficiency of the two types of private schools was not reported. Similarly, no data were collected on parental satisfaction or parental curriculum preferences, so it is not clear if the government-subsidized private schools were any more or less responsive to parental demand than their fully parent-funded counterparts. Both types of private schools outperformed government-run schools. See Ludger Wößmann, "Evidence on the Effects of Choice and Accountability from International Student Achievement Tests," Paper presented at the Cato Institute conference, "Looking Worldwide: What Americans Can Learn from School Choice in Other Countries," Washington, May 27, 2004.

29. Kingdon, "Private Schooling in India"; and Geeta Gandhi Kingdon, "The Quality and Efficiency of Private and Public Education: A Case Study of Urban India," *Oxford Bulletin of Economics and Statistics* 58, no. 1 (1996): 55–80.

30. Estelle James, Elizabeth M. King, and Ace Suryadi, "Finance, Management, and Costs of Public and Private Schools in Indonesia," *Economics of Education Review* 15, no. 4 (1996): 387–98.

31. For instance, the withholding of writing instruction by schools funded by some religious charities in early-19th-century England, on the purported grounds that it was "not necessary," but more likely because upward social mobility for the poor was feared as socially destabilizing by the upper classes of the time. See Coulson, *Market Education*, p. 88.

32. Milton Friedman, "The Role of Government in a Free Society," in *Capitalism and Freedom*, p. 32.

33. Friedman wrote in 1998: "I agree with a statement that Wilbur Cohen, former secretary of HEW under President Johnson, made in a 1972 debate with me on [Social] Security: 'A program that deals only with the poor will end up being a poor program.'" See Milton Friedman, "Freedom and School Vouchers," in Llewellyn H. Rockwell Jr., "Friedman v. Rockwell," *Chronicles*, December 1, 1998, http://www.mises.org/fullstory.aspx?control=92&month=12.

34. Andrew J. Coulson, "Forging Consensus," Mackinac Center for Public Policy, policy analysis, April 30, 2004, http://www.mackinac.org/article.asp?ID=6517.

35. Friedman, "The Role of Government in Education," p. 91.

36. See, for instance, John T. Wenders, "The Extent and Nature of Waste and Rent Dissipation in US Public Education," Paper presented for the Cato Institute Conference, "Creating a True Marketplace in Education," September 28, 2004. An earlier, abbreviated discussion of this issue by the same author appears online at

http://ocpathink.org/ViewPerspectiveEdition.asp?ID=23. See also Coulson, "How Markets Affect Quality."

37. Coulson, *Market Education*, chap. 6.

9. Discipline Is the Key to Milton Friedman's Gold Standard for Education Reform

John Merrifield

Milton Friedman's 1955 essay was the opening salvo in the modern intellectual and political struggle to level the education playing field for America's children. Friedman's treatment of education continued in *Capitalism and Freedom* (1962), *Free to Choose* (1980), and *Tyranny of the Status Quo* (1984).[1] Other scholars also questioned the role of government in education, but Friedman's command of logical, elegant, and accessible prose and good timing[2] gave his ideas unique staying power. The latest proof of that staying power is the present volume.

This essay focuses on the nexus between the intellectual and political battles over vouchers and examines how disciplined leadership can propel us to widespread adoption of Friedman's education reform "gold standard." The gold standard is Friedman's concept of vouchers in their purest form—government funding only for schooling "activities appropriate for the state to subsidize," especially the basic literacy and numeracy that have critical "neighborhood effects."[3] Subsidizing appropriate activities rather than institutions also means ending devastating government discrimination against private school users. The resulting level playing field for private and government-operated schools would generate the market accountability Friedman thought was essential for a least-cost, most-effective menu of schooling alternatives as diverse and dynamic as our children. I will explain the importance of Friedman's ideas about education reform, then discuss some key aspects of the ongoing school choice wars. Finally, I will suggest strategies for accelerating progress toward the Friedman vision of education reform, including ways to avoid catastrophic obstacles and detours.

Education Reform and Safeguarding Liberty

Thomas Jefferson, one of a very few policy analysts with an intellectual capacity comparable to Friedman's, said it clearly: "If a nation expects to be ignorant and free, it expects what never was and never will be."[4] Some people might argue that we've refuted Jefferson, that we are free even though our school system has left the majority of students without even basic skills, much less a grasp of key historical facts and core values. But we haven't refuted Jefferson, who was prescient about the necessary connection between education and liberty. We have already seen a considerable loss of freedom.[5] Certainly, we have inherited a strong Constitution, and our free enterprise tradition has considerable momentum, but without a literate, well-informed public we're just a talented demagogue away from the possibility of Third World–style tyranny and poverty. That is probably what former presidential adviser Hodding Carter meant by his reaction to recent findings of shocking ignorance among American children: "Ignorance about the basics of this free society is a danger to our nation's future."[6] Jefferson was quite aware of that calamitous risk: "Above all things I hope the education of the common people will be attended to; convinced that on their good sense we may rely with the most security for the preservation of a due degree of liberty."[7]

We can reclaim our lost liberties through a timely free enterprise transformation of our K–12 system. Free enterprise has been the tonic that has made us great, despite lagging sectors, such as education. The solution for lagging sectors is to subject them to the forces of discipline and innovation that prevail where free enterprise operates.

A national security perspective yields a current, concrete basis for concern. A 1959 book by Admiral Hyman Rickover blamed the education system for the dangerous difficulty of finding homegrown scientific talent: "The system looks upon talented children primarily as a vexing administrative problem."[8] Forty-two years later, the U.S. Commission on National Security observed that the K–12 problems remain a serious national security threat. Nobel laureate Leon Lederman also sees an impending economic crisis. "Our populations have never been more ignorant of science," writes Lederman. "If we don't fix our science and math educational system, the nation is really in deep trouble. Our economy has been surviving on immigration."[9]

By putting the interests of the current system's key stakeholders ahead of the interests of children, our political process has severely undermined the future of millions of children and put us in serious political and economic jeopardy. Both major wake-up calls of the last 50 years, the 1957 launch of two Soviet Sputnik satellites and the 1983 National Commission's "A Nation at Risk"[10] finding, prompted frenzied activity but few, if any, major improvements.

The current system's basic funding and governance process, and repeated futile attempts to significantly improve its performance and establish a high rate of steady progress, stands in defiance of all we know about the diversity of human beings, the political process, and human nature. We're beating a dead horse.[11] We've entrusted the content of schooling to the political process, truly a triumph of hope over experience. We have reams of evidence that incentives matter, but we entrust millions of children to a system with few, if any, incentives for educators to be efficient or innovative. We know that industries are more productive when competition prompts specialization in areas of strength, yet in linking school attendance to geographic location we eliminate competition and preclude even the little bit of specialization that political oversight of textbook selection, curriculum, and teacher training might permit. We know that children differ greatly in how they learn and what content provides them the greatest motivation to learn, but the political imperative to appear even-handed prompts us to school the vast majority of children in the same things by the same methods.

"A more informed citizenry"[12] would not tolerate an accountability process with such a solid theoretical and empirical basis for low expectations. In his 1955 essay, Friedman was already lamenting the "trend towards collectivism" and the "acceptance of whatever intervention that has already occurred as natural and unchangeable." As Jefferson pointed out, however, "if we think them [the people] not enlightened enough to exercise their control with a wholesome discretion, the remedy is not to take it from them, but to inform their discretion."[13] That means we have to educate the populace to improve our education system, a particularly difficult and urgent challenge.

The 50-state reform frenzy that followed the "Nation at Risk" report tested an exhaustive list of system-friendly reforms. Now we know that the Friedman gold standard is the only credible reform that does not already have a shameful record of expensive futility. An extensively documented version of that important message *needs* to reach a much wider audience.

Meeting the Challenge

Milton Friedman was aware of the magnitude of this challenge and did much more than define a policy objective. He also understood the transition stages needed to reach his gold standard of a minimal, properly focused, and neutral government role in education: "The voucher system we propose is a transition device intended to move you from where you are to where you would like to be, namely a system in which the government is not running any schools."[14] Two stages must precede the strictly private provision of schooling. Stage one is the implementation of a Friedman-style voucher program that would significantly reduce, even eliminate, private schools' current major competitive disadvantage, namely, having to sell something in a climate where a "free" alternative is offered. The second stage is the shakeout that would result from the competitive pressures unleashed by a Friedman-style voucher program.

Though the schooling needs of children, not funding demands of particular schools, justify school taxes, the public schools' longstanding public finance monopoly and assignment of children to neighborhood schools may still seem natural and unchangeable to many people. Therefore, informational lobbying may be insufficient to end the monopoly that forces private schools to sell services that are undercut by "free" public school offerings. It might require some modest choice programs to gradually change the public's definition of "public education" to mean a public commitment to school access rather than a system of government-operated schools. Government funding for private school users will attack the impression that public funds belong only to public school users, rather than to all children. At that point, it will become easier to make the case for child-based public funding of schooling at the same level regardless of which school parents chose. Friedman knew that once funding no longer substantially favored public school users, schools created by nimble entrepreneurs would gradually replace public schools in the areas with enough children to support a menu of school choices. In other words, on a level playing field, schools encumbered by politics and bureaucratic decisionmaking cannot compete with private schools.

In *Free to Choose*, Milton and Rose Friedman proposed that transformation of schooling eventually needs to go beyond privatization of provision to privatization of funding. They suggest that the benefits of ending government funding of K–12 schooling may be worth the possible reduction in the access of low-income families to schooling. The political feasibility of this especially controversial proposition will probably require confidence in philanthropy's willingness to generously underwrite the tuition of poor children. The less-controversial preceding stages of reform, in which the government would fund each child's schooling at the same level regardless of the school chosen, could help people understand and gain confidence that such a system could work.

The energizing effects of free enterprise, parents topping off public funding with their own money—private add-ons—when they pick a school that charges more than the public funds, plus political competition for scarce public funds could gradually raise the importance of the add-on share of tuition. According to Richard Vedder, this is exactly what appears to be happening at many state universities. State money covers a rapidly falling share of total spending. In such a scenario in K–12 education, the electorate may let government funding shrink because money from other sources, including private add-ons and charitable donations, keeps growth in the add-on share of tuition from reducing the choices of the poor.[15] Such a dynamic could eventually yield a statewide school system with no government funding, or only limited indirect funding through a nonrefundable tax credit system like the one outlined by Andrew Coulson.[16]

Nevertheless, I have my doubts about the political feasibility of this route to total school-state separation. The dynamics of add-ons gradually replacing government funds is uncertain. Philanthropic funds may not on their own be enough to support poor children adequately, and capital market imperfections might threaten young middle-class families with a huge cash-flow problem. Absent the availability of inexpensive long-term loans for education expenses, families would expect huge tuition expenses in their earliest, lowest-earning years. Still, despite the shortcomings of a scenario in which add-ons gradually displace state funding, the Friedman transition strategy of first eliminating discrimination against private school users, followed by the virtual abandonment of government-provided schooling, is the most plausible political route to separation of school and state.

Status of and Prospects for the Friedman Gold Standard

To realize the key benefits of free enterprise, the transformation of our education system must eliminate government discrimination against private school users. In other words, roughly the same amount of public funding must support a particular child regardless of who owns and operates the school he attends. That, plus freedom to add on, low entry barriers, and market determination of schooling practices, will "give full play to entrepreneurial initiative."[17] If we make it that far, I am confident that we will achieve, at least, Friedman's vision of privatization of school provision.

Theory-based arguments, evidence from ancient competitive school systems,[18] and evidence from other industries may not win implementation of a Friedman-style voucher program. Hard "evidence" and experience gained from some working voucher programs may be needed. That most people have never even heard of vouchers,[19] much less understand the potentially huge differences among voucher programs, signifies that existing efforts have yet to reach a wide audience, and the misinformed remain an even bigger challenge than the ignorant.

What constitutes relevant evidence? Today's existing voucher programs are quite limited in scale and scope and thus have little more than a word in common with a universal Friedman-style program. Given the difficulty, not only of changing the public's deeply ingrained impressions about what "public education" means, but also of refuting what a misinformed subpopulation believes about vouchers, there are two potential approaches to pursue. One is to focus an information-lobbying campaign in the one or few states most likely to adopt a Friedman-style voucher program. Such a campaign must include an attack on fallacies, including correcting the misunderstanding of the effects of limited programs. Arguably, major recent efforts have taken place in states least likely to adopt such a program, or the object of the campaign has fallen far short of a Friedman-style program, or both. Concentrating resources and attention where total success is most likely is thus one possible strategy for moving forward.

The other approach is incremental and would likely reduce opposition by avoiding harder-to-understand radical change. An incremental approach would likely limit vouchers to the current system's worst victims. Such a strategy may eventually yield the desired Friedman-style voucher program or an equivalent tax credit program, but it is fraught with danger. Targeted programs certainly provide some immediate relief to the participants, and they sometimes yield modest systemwide benefits.[20] Such programs also energize choice advocates with a sense of genuine accomplishment. Media scrutiny of especially bad schools and modest rivalry pressures prompt some improvements, and the publicity raises the general comfort level with school choice strategies that might otherwise be seen as novel and suspect. Nevertheless, *successful* limited programs will beget additional limited programs, and the incrementalism dynamic does not typically move toward fewer restrictions leading to more broadly based programs. Certainly, the tightening regulation of charter schools seems the latest demonstration of what was already known in Jefferson's time, that government programs tend to acquire restrictions rather than shed them: "The natural progress of things is for liberty to yield and government to gain ground."[21] Evan Osborne's contemporary empirical findings on economic policy reform make the same point: "Overall the evidence strongly indicates the superiority of radical reform. Gradual reform may not hold, perhaps because interest groups negatively affected by it are able to mobilize to defeat it due to the modest [initial] gains."[22] Or, what the Center for Education Reform observed about charter legislation—"It is harder to change than to get it right the first time."[23]—may hold true in the case of voucher programs as well.

Pilot programs guarantee huge delays without any assurance that they will generate insightful data or more radical reform. Pseudoexperiments jeopardize proposed reforms by misrepresenting their effects. Alleged experiments are especially risky when politicians, not scientists, have the final word on design issues. All three concerns apply to the current programs widely called voucher "experiments," though most were not set up as experiments. Delay is very costly. We are already "a nation at risk." The alleged experiments are too small to yield a telling evaluation of transformational Friedman-style voucher programs. It could take decades to demonstrate that helping a few economically disadvantaged children with narrowly targeted programs will not produce significant widespread educational improvements. If choice advocates call them experiments, lackluster results will erode the political feasibility of choice-based transformational reform through guilt by association. Another decade of the minimal returns that are inevitable when limited trial programs carry too many restrictions *may* be enough to mislead the public into believing that parental choice is an ineffective reform catalyst.

The political struggle to implement narrowly targeted programs as alleged experiments has widely typecast parental choice as just an escape hatch. I am no longer surprised, but still appalled, when someone assumes that school choice programs cannot effect real systemic reform. Examples like this one from Jonathan Kozol are common: Parental choice is "an escape hatch for a few students, instead of a way to improve the school system."[24] Unwarranted hype, reckless generalization, and undisciplined pursuit of "choice" are largely responsible for this major obstacle to the Friedman gold standard. The limited voucher measures occasionally produced by the political battle sidetrack key intellectual battles with alleged evidence that is often wrong, misleading, or irrelevant.

Furthermore, limited pilot programs sanctify the key elements of the existing, dysfunctional system. If proclaimed policy experiments entail moving relatively few children, often only poor children or children in the worst schools, we signal to the public that most of the existing schools remain a good deal for most of the students. Nothing could be further from the truth.

Achieving a Highly Disciplined Implementation Stage

Even if every organization that advocates choice recognizes that limited programs are not reform catalysts, and that they might endanger the transformation cause, the political process will still produce limited programs. The challenge, therefore, is to produce a disciplined strategy to maximize the beneficial aspects of such programs and minimize their potentially huge costs.

We should leave compromise to the politicians. Since lobbying for limited programs does not significantly diminish the opposition, we should lobby only for programs that will give "full play to entrepreneurial initiative."[25] This approach properly defines the scope of the K–12 problem and will clearly outline what school reform through expanded choice entails. It may take some time to achieve the Friedman gold standard, but the efforts to enact it will establish what choice advocates stand for and will focus the public debate on proposals capable of effecting the transformation needed by a "nation at risk." We can implement a definite policy outcome in stages if necessary, but we should not seek it in stages.

This strategy does not preclude supporting the escape hatch programs produced by political compromise. Escape hatches provide some immediate gains for some children, and they erode inaccurate and counterproductive stereotypes about "public education." Escape hatches also attack misconceptions about some effects of choice, and supporting them avoids alienating potential political allies. Demand for escape hatches at least reminds policymakers that the "comprehensive uniformity"[26] that results from the political process cannot effectively serve a diverse student population.

Staying focused on system transformation will be difficult. Choice advocates must diplomatically explain that stymieing the positive effects of genuine competition by targeting certain children hurts everyone, including even the targeted children. Especially devastating are rules like price control and participation caps aimed at keeping the "rich" from benefiting. Notwithstanding concerns about providing unnecessary benefits for the rich, there just aren't enough people matching the rich person stereotype of a free-spending fat cat to warrant drastic limitations in otherwise promising reforms. Ninety-five percent of American households earn less than $126,525 a year.[27] Government discrimination against private school users is a trivial issue only for superrich families for whom education costs only a small share of disposable income. As Milton Friedman has said, programs for the poor become poor programs.[28]

The Friedman gold standard would improve the school choices of all but a tiny number of superrich families. Because of frequent stories about the truly horrific conditions in the worst schools, and because the truth about the system is so bad, much of the public, including many education analysts, lives in something approaching denial. The nation is at risk because excellent schools are rare, even in affluent suburbs. Failure to maintain the focus on achieving the Friedman gold standard would reinforce debilitating fallacies about the nature of the K–12 problem.

Especially harmful is the failure to strongly resist labels like "pilot" and "experiment" for programs incapable of producing useful insights about programs that would give "full play to entrepreneurial initiative." That was true before there were any voucher programs. It is especially true now that we have extensive information about the effects of limited programs.

When a study of limited programs finds modest benefits (which is the norm), we have to treat the modest benefits as an opportunity to highlight how even a little competitive rivalry generates some positive "competition" effects. We then have to get people to imagine the benefits that would arise if we had full market accountability in schooling. If we can get noteworthy benefits from moving just a few kids to the better schools within the existing system, just think what we could accomplish with genuine market pressure, pressure that allows for the emergence of new schools that stimulate the entire system to improve. Since competition per se is often deemed contrary to the desirable values of education, we have to repeatedly connect it with the improvements sought by the public and reiterate that those improvements won't happen without genuine market competition.

Disciplined implementation of a Friedman-style voucher program must also include effective attacks on counterproductive stereotypes. Some schools are much better than others, but because the current system rests on so many fallacies, very few existing schools are even adequate, much less close to what they could be for the money that they spend. Until we explode the myth that most schools are fine— a myth reinforced by the well-intentioned efforts of many choice advocates—many people will vote against changes that might affect their school, which means they will oppose the very reforms capable of effecting genuine systemic change.

A major theme of implementation must be that giving "full play to entrepreneurial initiative" doesn't mean just a larger and slightly improved version of the private sector we have now. Even without the entrepreneurial explosion that would result from the voucherization of existing public funding, pressure to compete and opportunities to specialize would transform the menu of choices available through just the existing schools.

Many of the objections against restriction-laden programs do not apply to the Friedman gold standard. For example, teachers have some genuine basis for concern about limited programs, which may yield more jobs in lower-paying private schools and fewer in higher-paying ones. But ending discrimination against private school users would greatly improve private schools' ability to compete for teachers, and market accountability would foster the professional autonomy that teaching professionals need and crave.

Limited programs can also impose additional costs on existing programs.[29] The Friedman gold standard, on the contrary, would ultimately eliminate many of the costs of the status quo. By cutting administrative budgets and allowing private add-ons, it would yield additional funds for teacher salaries. That is exactly where school operators would have to increase spending to compete for students. In such a climate, excellent teachers would likely command highly competitive salaries.

The Friedman gold standard has another key virtue. It produces the child-based funding equity that continues to be an elusive and costly goal of funding equalization lawsuits. The focus on the unbiased funding of children rather than on schools would allow politicians to avoid apologies for impacts on the current system. The resulting choice-based system will be the one that best serves a diverse student population. The focus on student welfare reduces potential confusion about goals and avoids feeding suspicions that education freedom is really a scheme with effects to be downplayed.

Limited programs might promote stratification because most of the choices are slightly better or worse versions of uniform offerings, and the wealthiest applicants will win the bidding war to attend the best schools. Through incentives that push schools to specialize in popular subjects and teaching methods, the Friedman gold standard will foster ethnic, racial, and income diversity of the school population. Use of rented space, transfers of ownership of school buildings, and new construction will allow new schools to spread successful practices and make waiting lists temporary, and then rare.

Limited evidence and survey data suggest that greater freedom to choose will greatly expand secular education options. Child-based funding is not de facto government support of religious institutions as alleged by supporters of the minority opinion in the *Zelman* case heard before the U.S. Supreme Court in 2002 and by the Blaine Amendments in state constitutions.

Conclusion

In the end, successful implementation of what I have called Friedman's "gold standard" for education reform will be a demonstration, not an experiment. Market accountability already has an impressive track record, even in education. Writing in the *Washington Post* in 1995, Friedman expressed his continuing hope: "I sense that we are on the verge of a breakthrough in one state or another, which will then sweep like wildfire through the rest of the country."[30] The emergence of a competitive education industry in some locale will be the modern demonstration that ignites the "wildfire" that spreads genuine education reform throughout much of the world. Milton Friedman defined the destination and provided some directions and mileposts. There is an enormous amount at stake, so let us hope and pray that we are on the shortest road to that outcome, and that we do not stall or carelessly lose our way.

Notes

1. Milton Friedman, *Capitalism and Freedom* (Chicago: University of Chicago Press, 1962); Milton and Rose Friedman, *Free to Choose* (Orlando: Harcourt, 1980); Milton and Rose Friedman, *Tyranny of the Status Quo* (Orlando: Harcourt, 1984); and Milton and Rose D. Friedman, *Two Lucky People* (Chicago: University of Chicago Press, 1998).

2. See R. Flesch, *Why Johnny Can't Read and What You Can Do about It* (New York: Harper & Row, 1955); and Hyman G. Rickover, *Education and Freedom* (New York: E.P. Dutton, 1959).

3. Milton Friedman, "The Role of Government in Education," in *Economics and the Public Interest,* ed. R. A. Solo (New Brunswick, NJ: Rutgers University Press, 1955).

4. Thomas Jefferson, Letter to Charles Yancey, 1816, http://etext.virginia.edu/ jefferson/quotations/jeff1350htm.

5. See James Bovard, *Freedom in Chains* (New York: St. Martins, 1999); and Milton Friedman, "We Have Socialism, QED," *The Margin,* September–October 1990.

6. See Jimmy Moore, "Survey Finds Students Ignorant of Basic First Amendment Rights," *Talon News,* February 1, 2005; and the education section of U.S. Commission on National Security/21st Century, *Road Map for National Security: Imperative for Change,* Phase III report, 2001.

7. Thomas Jefferson, Letter to James Madison, 1787, http://etext.virginia.edu/ jefferson/quotations/jeff 1350htm.http://etext.virginia.edu/jefferson/quotations/ jeff1350.htm.

8. Rickover.

9. Cited in John Merrow, "Unlearning Bad Science," *Education Week,* February 23, 2005, pp. 56, 40.

10. National Commission on Excellence in Education, "A Nation at Risk: The Imperative for Educational Reform," U.S. Department of Education, 1983.

11. See Myron Lieberman, *Public Education: An Autopsy* (Cambridge, MA: Harvard University Press, 1993); and "The Horse Story," http://www.rh.edu/~schroth/ dead%20horse.htm.

12. Mancur Olson, quoted in Lieberman, p. 160.

13. Thomas Jefferson, Letter to William C. Jarvis, 1820, http://etext.virginia.edu/ jefferson/quotations/jeff1350htm.

14. Milton Friedman, Letter to John Merrifield, August 12, 1996.

15. See Richard Vedder, *Going Broke by Degree: Why College Costs Too Much* (Washington: AEI Press, 2004).

16. Andrew Coulson, "Toward Market Education: Are Vouchers or Tax Credits the Better Path?" Cato Institute Policy Analysis no. 392, February 22, 2001.

17. Milton Friedman, e-mail to Gary Hoover, March 31, 2003.

18. Andrew Coulson, *Market Education: The Unknown History* (New Brunswick, NJ: Transaction, 1999).

19. See Terry Moe, *Schools, Vouchers, and the American Public* (Washington: Brookings Institution Press, 2001).

20. Mark Harrison, *Education Matters: Government, Markets, and New Zealand Schools* (Wellington: Education Forum, 2004).

21. Thomas Jefferson, Letter to E. Carrington, May 27, 1787, http://etext.virginia.edu/jefferson/quotations/jeff1800htm.

22. Evan Osborne, "Measuring Bad Governance," *Cato Journal* 23, no. 3 (Winter 2004): 415.

23. Center for Education Reform, "May Education Reform Report," 2000, www.edreform.org.

24. Quoted in Troy Segal, "Saving Our Schools," *Business Week*, September 14, 1992, pp. 70–78. For more examples, see John Merrifield, *The School Choice Wars* (Lanham, MD: Scarecrow Education Press, 2001), pp. 23, 35–38.

25. Friedman, e-mail to Hoover.

26. Byron W. Brown, "Why Governments Run Schools," *Economics of Education Review* 11, no. 4 (1992): 287–300.

27. Tax Foundation, "2002 Tax Data by Income Class," http://www.taxfoundation.org/prtopincome.html.

28. Robert Kuttner, "Agreeing to Disagree," Interview with Milton Friedman, *American Prospect*, July 2006.

29. Henry M. Levin and Cyrus E. Driver, "Costs of an Education Voucher System," *Education Economics* 5, no. 3 (December 1997): 265–83.

30. Milton Friedman, "Public Schools: Make Them Private," op-ed, *Washington Post*, February 19, 1995.

10. From Universal to Targeted Vouchers: The Relevance of the Friedmans' Proposals for Developing Countries

James Tooley

Introduction: From 1955 to 1980

Fifty years ago Milton Friedman not only wrote "The Role of Government in Education," but he also visited India for the first time and was "introduced," as he puts it, to a "step down from dire poverty."[1] That chronological coincidence provides the pretext, if one is needed, to focus on the overlap between the Friedmans' ideas on the role of government in schooling and what is happening in education in developing countries today. I will be reading Milton Friedman's 1955 seminal contribution to this field in conjunction with its elaboration in Milton and Rose Friedman's *Free to Choose*, published in 1980.[2] Important modifications are made in the later work that provide the springboard for the discussion here.

In 1955 Milton Friedman wrote in favor of education vouchers, satisfied that their justification rested on the "neighborhood effects" argument.[3] Educating a child, he argued, brings gains not only to the child and parents but also to others, "promoting a stable and democratic society." This provides a reasonable argument for compulsory education. Moreover, while suggesting that "it might be both feasible and desirable to require the parents to meet the costs directly," if special provision were made for the minority that could not afford them, Friedman also acknowledges that universal public funding may be a desirable companion to compulsory education.[4] The argument for universal public funding, rather than "special provision" for only the economically disadvantaged, seemed to Friedman to turn on two critical considerations. First, families vary in their resources; second, the standard of education required by the state involves "very sizable costs."[5] Those two reasons, combined

139

with the neighborhood effects argument, led Friedman to propose vouchers as a means of enhancing the education market within the constraints of public compulsion and funding.

By 1980 the views of Friedman and his wife, Rose, had changed: they were no longer convinced about the "justification for . . . compulsory attendance."[6] Important to that change of mind was the historical research of, among others, the late E. G. West, who first published his important book, *Education and the State*, 10 years after Friedman's original essay. West's research was inspired in part as a challenge to Milton Friedman's voucher proposal.[7] The Friedmans observed that research "on the history of schooling in the United States, the United Kingdom, and other countries has persuaded us that compulsory attendance at schools is not necessary to achieve that minimum standard of literacy and knowledge." Research had shown that schooling was "well-nigh universal in the United States before attendance was required," and in the United Kingdom, it was "well-nigh universal before either compulsory attendance or government financing of schooling existed."[8] That evidence challenged the desirability of compulsory schooling laws, and hence, as compulsion was a prime justification for public funding, the raison d'être of the latter began to disintegrate.

Although still viewing the education voucher as a useful stepping stone, by 1980 the Friedmans were inclined toward something more radical: "We regard the voucher plan as a partial solution because it affects neither the financing of schooling nor the compulsory attendance laws. *We favor going much farther*."[9] "Farther," in this case, was a move away from the desirability of universal vouchers to an emphasis on, at most, targeted vouchers: "Public financing of hardship cases might remain, but that is a far different matter than having the government finance a school system for 90 percent of the children going to school because 5 or 10 percent of them might be hardship cases."[10]

By 1980, then, the Friedmans seem to have been in favor of a more complete privatization of education, with government abandoning compulsory schooling laws and withdrawing from the funding of education, except for, at most, a small minority of parents who are "hardship cases." The Friedmans did not further elaborate on the theme of privatization, acknowledging that their views "on financing and attendance laws will appear to most readers to be extreme" and conceding their pragmatic "return to the voucher proposal—a much more moderate departure from present practice."[11]

Private Schools for the Poor

I want to explore this more radical departure in the context of developing countries and more specifically in relation to the education of low-income families there. Recent research suggests that this more radical approach set aside by the Friedmans might actually have the greatest purchase in some of the poorest countries on earth. This prospect might seem surprising to some readers, for even the Friedmans themselves had observed that outright privatization would be easier to justify "the wealthier a society and the more evenly distributed is income within it."[12]

By contrast, something remarkable is happening in many, perhaps all, developing countries. Private schools that cater to the poor are "mushrooming" in urban slums and shantytowns and in rural villages. Such schools charge very low fees—perhaps $1 to $3 per month, making them affordable to laborers, market traders, peasant farmers, and fishermen. I first came across that phenomenon in a serendipitous "discovery" of private schools in the slums of Hyderabad, India, while taking time off from consultancy work evaluating an elite private college for the World Bank. Since then my teams have been conducting research in India, China, Ghana, Nigeria, and Kenya, combing selected poor urban and rural areas to locate private schools, analyzing their extent, and comparing them with government alternatives.[13] As the existence of private schools for the poor may be unfamiliar to some readers, let me present a picture of the type of place where my research teams have been finding private schools.

Hyderabad, India

Visit the ultramodern high-rise development of "High Tech City" and you'll see why Hyderabad dubs itself "Cyberabad," proud of its position at the forefront of India's technological revolution. Cross the river Musi into the "Old City," however, and proceed toward the Charminar, the 16th-century triumphal arch, and you'll see a different India, more akin to the India Milton Friedman first observed in 1955: congested narrow streets weaving their way through crowded markets and densely populated slums. For our survey, we covered three zones in the Old City—Bandlaguda, Bhadurpura, and Charminar—with a population of about 800,000, covering an area of 30 square kilometers, and including about 22 percent of the total population of Hyderabad. We included only schools that were in "slums," as defined in the latest available census, areas that lacked amenities such as indoor plumbing, running water, electricity, and paved roads.

In the slums of Hyderabad, a typical private school is found in a converted house, in a small alleyway behind bustling and noisy streets, or above a shop. A large signboard with bold painted letters will be posted above the large metal gate; you must stoop to enter the courtyard that serves as a playground and assembly gathering area. Once you are inside, the classrooms are often rather dark, by Western standards, with no doors hung in the doorways, and noise from the streets outside can be heard everywhere, entering through barred but unglazed windows. Walls are painted white but discolored by pollution, heat, and the general wear and tear of the children; no pictures or work is hung on them. Children will usually be in school uniform, and although class sizes are small, the rooms will seem crowded. Often the top floor of the building will have construction work going on, to increase the number of classrooms. The school proprietor will usually live in a couple of rooms at the back of the house.

Of 918 schools found in the three zones, only 35 percent were government operated, compared to 23 percent "recognized" and 37 percent "unrecognized" private unaided schools—that is, there were more unrecognized private than government schools. ("Recognized" or, in other countries, "registered," signifies that the school has applied to be inspected for conformance with state standards.) Five percent of the total schools were private aided. With 100 percent of teachers' salaries funded by government, private aided schools are not recognizably different from public schools. In terms of student enrollment, 65 percent of school children were found to be attending private unaided schools. Roughly the same percentage of children was found in the unrecognized private schools and in government schools (23 percent compared to 24 percent). In these poor areas of India, then, the vast majority of schoolchildren attend private school.[14]

Fees for those schools are very low. Average tuition in recognized private schools at first grade, for instance, is about $2.12 per month, while in the unrecognized schools it was about $1.51. The expected earnings of the type of father who would send his children to these schools would be about $30 per month—so fees could approach about 7 percent of monthly earnings. For the poorest children, however, the schools frequently provide scholarships or subsidized places. Our research found that 7 percent of children were provided with free places, and 11 percent paid reduced fees. In effect, the poor are subsidizing access to private education for the poorest.[15]

The Old City of Hyderabad is predominantly Muslim, but that does not mean that the private schools are religious. Legally, private schools must be managed by a society or trust (including religious organizations). However, we found only three (1.0 percent) unrecognized and one (0.5 percent) recognized private schools run by religious societies. The vast majority are managed by a secular society, to meet legal requirements, although, in effect, they are run by a husband-and-wife team of proprietors, who themselves come from the poor communities served. These private schools are not the madrasas feared by some in America.

Interestingly, when Milton Friedman was writing seven years after his first 1955 visit to India, he noted that "hope for India lies not in the exceptional Tatas or similar giants, but precisely in the hole-in-the-wall firms, in the small- and medium-sized enterprises ... in the millions of small entrepreneurs who line the streets of every city with their sometimes minuscule shops and workshops."[16] It is precisely those "hole-in-the-wall" educational entrepreneurs—edupreneurs—who are providing the foundations for an emerging education industry in India today.

Other Selected Countries

Those findings are not isolated. Our research has extended beyond India into other sites as diverse as Ga, Ghana; Gansu, China; and Kibera, Kenya. In the poor fishing villages, subsistence farms, and large industrial dormitory towns of the Ga district in Ghana, our researchers found 799 schools in total, of which 25 percent were government (197 schools), compared to 23 percent (177) unregistered and 52 percent (405) registered private schools. In total, 64 percent of school students were found in private schools, with 15 percent in unregistered private schools, compared to 36 percent in government schools. Again, the majority of children in this poor area attend private school. Although fees of unregistered private schools here could approach 10 percent of a family's monthly earnings, many of the poorest schools have responded by allowing *daily* fees to be paid, so that a poor fisherman could send his daughter to school on the days he had funds. Such flexibility was not possible in the public schools that demanded full payment of their "levies" before the term started.

Gansu Province, China, situated on the upper and middle reaches of the Yellow River in northwestern China, is home to 25 million people. More than 75 percent of Gansu's population is rural, with illiteracy rates among people aged 15 and older of nearly 20 percent for men and 40 percent for women. Roughly half of Gansu's rural counties (41) are nationally designated as "impoverished." Our research teams found 586 private schools for the poor in the impoverished villages. The vast majority—99.5 percent—of the private schools are run by individuals or the villages themselves and depend almost entirely on student tuition fees. Public schools also charge fees but, of course, receive state funding as well. At all levels, the private school fees were usually slightly lower than those charged by the public schools. Average fees charged for first grade in elementary school were RMB 68.79 (about $8.33) per semester, compared to RMB 70.7 (about $8.56) in the public schools. Those differences may not be insignificant to someone living on $125 per year. But the main reason why parents chose to send their children to private schools was because the public schools supposedly made available to them were simply too inaccessible—often requiring a multihour journey on foot through inhospitable terrain.

Kibera, Kenya, is the largest slum in Sub-Saharan Africa. Estimates of population range from 500,000 to 800,000 nestled into an area of about 630 acres. Mud-walled, corrugated-iron-roofed settlements huddle along the old Uganda Railway for several miles and crowd along steep narrow mud tracks, until Kibera reaches the posh suburbs. In Nairobi's two rainy seasons, the mud tracks become mud baths. In this setting, we found 76 private elementary and high schools, enrolling 12,132 students. The schools were typically run by local "educational entrepreneurs," a third of whom were women, who had seen the possibility of making a living from running a school, as well as recognized the demand for private education in the slums. Many again offered free places to the poorest, including orphans.

144

Kenya gained worldwide attention in 2003 when, with great fanfare and a $55 million grant from the World Bank, it introduced Free Primary Education. Former U.S. president Bill Clinton, when asked by anchorman Peter Jennings on ABC's *Primetime* which one living person he would most like to meet, said President Kibaki of Kenya, "because he has abolished school fees," which "would affect more lives than any president had done or would ever do by the end of this year." In fact, the success of the policy may be quite mixed. Our research on the effects of FPE on enrollment trends points to a net decline in attendance at any school of nearly 8,000 children from one slum alone! Clearly, those figures are based on the decline reported by school owners and may be subject to exaggeration. Nevertheless, whatever the precise figures, they clearly point to the possibility that government and international intervention has had the effect of crowding out private enterprise.[17]

Development Experts and the Quality of Schools for the Poor

When I first "discovered" for myself the existence of private schools for the poor, I assumed that development experts didn't know about them and that bringing the phenomenon to their attention would make them think differently about the Friedmans' fundamental concern, the role of government in education, applied to developing countries. It was one thing to argue that universal elementary education required huge dollops of international aid to public schooling if one thought that was the only option available, but once the existence of a vibrant private sector serving (as we found in many cases) a majority of poor children was pointed out, I assumed this must make a huge difference to the options to be considered. I was wrong. It turned out that my discovery was not a discovery at all; it was something actually quite well-known by at least some development experts. But it was something that was curiously played down when it came to policy implications.

The *Oxfam Education Report* is typical.[18] Played down as far as any significance is concerned is the observation that "it is interesting to note that a lower-cost private sector has emerged to meet the demands of poor households." Indeed, there is "a growing market for private education among poor households"; "private education is a far more pervasive fact of life than is often recognised."[19] Surprisingly, the fact that the poor are helping themselves in this way gains no mention in the conclusions, which state the standard response of development educationalists, that there can be hope, but only if countries, rich and poor alike, renew their commitment to "free and compulsory" public education.[20]

The same experts also seem to accept that the reason why poor parents are sending their children to private schools is the gross inadequacies of state education. Again, the *Oxfam Education Report* is typical: it is the "inadequacies of public education systems" that have "driven many poor households into private systems." Most important is the problem of teacher absenteeism and commitment. The author, Kevin Watkins, is candid: ". . . there is no doubting the *appalling standard of provision in public education* across much of the developing world."[21]

So, why aren't development experts applauding poor parents who exit the "appalling" state schools and send their children to private schools? Why aren't they thinking along the lines of the Friedmans' radical proposal—of "targeted" vouchers for those too poor to access private schools, perhaps only a minority of the disadvantaged in urban areas, who are currently stuck in totally inadequate state schools? The explicit reason given is that the private schools for the poor are of an *even lower* quality than the public schools; indeed, it is charged that they "offer a low-quality service" that is so bad it will "restrict children's future opportunities."[22] The claim of low-quality private provision for the poor is commonplace, but it doesn't seem to be based on any evidence. The *Oxfam Education Report* itself is up front that there is little or no evidence either way: "Surprisingly, in view of the confident assertions made in some quarters, there is little hard evidence to substantiate the view that private schools systematically outperform public schools with comparable levels of resourcing."[23]

A priori it is claimed that private schools must be of lower quality, for they employ untrained teachers who are paid much less than their government counterparts, and that buildings and facilities are grossly inadequate. Both of those facts are largely true, but does that mean that private schools are inferior—particularly against the weight of parental preferences to the contrary? One Ghanaian school owner challenged me when I observed that her school building was little more than a corrugated iron roof on rickety poles and that the government school, just a few hundred yards away, was a smart new school building. "Education is not about buildings," she scolded. "What matters is what is in the teacher's heart. In our hearts, we love the children and do our best for them." She left it open, when probed, what the teachers in the government school felt in their hearts for the poor children.

We took the issue of the relative quality of private and public schools seriously, using both observational and student achievement data to explore it. Our researchers first called unannounced at schools and asked for a tour, noted what teachers were doing, made an inventory of facilities, and administered detailed questionnaires.

Certainly, it was true that in some countries the facilities of the private schools were markedly inferior to those of the public schools. In China, where researchers were asked to locate a public school in the village nearest to where they had found a private school for comparison purposes—often many miles away—private school facilities were generally worse than those publicly provided. That was predictable, given that the private schools slightly undercut the public ones in terms of fees and served the poorest villages where there were no public schools. At the other end of the spectrum, however, in Hyderabad, on every input, including the provision of blackboards, playgrounds, desks, drinking water, toilets, and separate toilets for boys and girls, both types of private unaided schools—recognized and unrecognized—were superior to the government schools.

When it came to the key question of whether or not teaching was going on in the classrooms, both types of private schools were superior to the public schools in all cases except China, where there was no statistically significant difference between the two school types. In Hyderabad, when researchers called unannounced on the classrooms, in only 75 percent of the government schools was teaching taking place, compared to 98 percent of the recognized and 91 percent of the unrecognized private schools. In Delhi, in only 38 percent of government schools was there teaching going on, compared to around 70 percent of private recognized and unrecognized schools. Finally, in Ga, Ghana, 57 percent of teachers were teaching in government schools, compared to 66 percent and 75 percent in unregistered and registered private schools, respectively.

To compare the achievement of students in public and private schools in each location where we conducted research, we first grouped schools by size and management type. We then took random samples of the fourth or fifth grade elementary school children in each group. In all, we tested a total of roughly 2,000 to 4,000 students in each location in English, mathematics, state languages in India and Kenya, and religious and moral education and social studies, respectively, in Ghana and Nigeria. All children were also given IQ tests, as were their teachers. Finally, questionnaires were distributed to children, their parents, teachers, and school managers, seeking information on family backgrounds.

Our analysis of those data has not yet been published. However, for the record, in all cases analyzed so far—Ghana (Ga), India (Hyderabad, Mahbubnagar, and Delhi), and Nigeria (Lagos)—students in private schools achieved at higher levels than did their counterparts in government schools. Most important, once the data are controlled for a rich array of characteristics of the students, their families, the resources available at their schools, and the process of school choice itself, the achievement gap is maintained in favor of the private schools. If these findings withstand the scrutiny of our academic peers, it will be possible to say with some confidence that it is not the case that private schools serving low-income families are inferior to those provided by the state. Significantly, in all cases analyzed, even the unrecognized schools—those that are dismissed by the development experts as being obviously of poor quality—outperform their public counterparts.

Implications of the Radical Friedman Solution

In 1955 Friedman wrote that the time had come "to re-examine the existing activities of government and to make a fresh assessment of the activities that are and those that are not justified."[24] In 2005 we can say that the time is ripe to make a similarly fresh assessment of justification for the role of government in education in developing countries, combining new evidence with the analytical techniques employed by the Friedmans.

We have seen that, often hidden from view of the development experts or swept under the carpet as an embarrassing irrelevance, private schools for the poor are "mushrooming." In the urban and peri-urban[25] areas we surveyed, private schools provide a substantial majority of schooling for the poor. In rural areas, they may provide a substantial minority of schooling. Charging very low, affordable fees, private schools are emerging that cater to some of the poorest people on this planet. Contrary to the assumptions of development experts, if our results withstand scrutiny, it is not the case that these mushrooming private schools are of low quality. In fact, they seem to be superior to state schools in terms of attainment in key curriculum areas.

What are the implications of these findings? I believe that, just as the Friedmans were influenced by the evidence of history, the empirical findings from contemporary developing countries might lead to a reconsideration of the Friedmans' more radical proposal for a more complete privatization of education coupled with "targeted vouchers" for the most disadvantaged, especially in developing countries. Before moving on to discuss these implications, we might also explore the implications for debates over education policy in highly developed nations such as America.

First, it is clear that the evidence from developing countries today can help challenge at least two of the objections that the Friedmans noted concerning the introduction of education vouchers in America. One of those fundamental objections they characterized as "doubt about new schools."[26] Given that private schools were then either "parochial schools or elite academies," critics of the voucher proposal wanted to know what reason there was "to suppose that alternatives will really arise." The Friedmans were convinced that "a market would develop where it does not exist today . . . attract-[ing] many entrants, both from public schools and from other occupations." Their conviction came from talking to many people about vouchers: "We have been impressed by the number of persons who said something like, 'I have always wanted to teach [or run a school] but I couldn't stand the education bureaucracy, red tape, and general ossification of the public schools. Under your plan, I'd like to try my hand at starting a school.'"[27]

The evidence from developing countries today supports the Friedmans' confidence in the entrepreneurial spirit; in developing countries, at least, educational entrepreneurs *do* emerge to provide educational opportunities, even for some of the poorest members of society. They emerge because parents and poor communities are concerned about education; it is a fundamental priority. When they have (well-founded) doubts about the efficiency and effectiveness of public schools, they'll create alternatives of their own.

Evidence from developing countries also might help challenge another of the fundamental objections to vouchers in America, that prosperous families would "top up," or supplement, the state provision with their own funds. The Friedmans call this the "economic class issue."[28] Critics argued that topping up vouchers would penalize poor parents who wouldn't want to spend their resources on education. The Friedmans replied that "this view . . . seems to us another example of the tendency of intellectuals to denigrate parents who are poor. Even the very poorest can—and do—scrape up a few extra dollars to improve the quality of their children's schooling, although they cannot replace the whole of the present cost of public schooling."[29] The evidence from developing countries supports this argument: if some of the poorest parents on this planet will scrimp and save to pay for their children's education, is it plausible that the same could not be true of the comparatively affluent "poor" in America today?

Clearly, the evidence from developing countries goes further than that. It suggests that many poor parents can in fact pay for the whole of their children's schooling, without any assistance from government. This brings us to the Friedmans' radical solution of a more thorough privatization. For what we are seeing in Africa and Asia, in effect, is a grass-roots privatization of education. That raises the possibility that we may not be too radical but rather too cautious if we look only to state intervention through vouchers to assist the poor. The poor in Asia and Africa don't sit idly by, dispossessed and disenfranchised—adjectives used by the liberal elite to describe the disadvantaged in America—acquiescent in their government's failure until outsiders step in to better their lot. Instead, some of the most disadvantaged people on this planet engage in self-help: they vote with their feet, exit the public schools, and move their children to private schools set up by educational entrepreneurs from their own communities to cater to their needs without any outside help. Could it be that the government intervention we take for granted in America crowds out parallel educational enterprise that could help the poor to help themselves, as they are doing in places like Kenya and Ghana and Hyderabad, India? Could it be that real privatization could emerge in the same way it has emerged in developing countries, from the bottom up?

There may be sufficient differences between America today and developing countries to preclude such a possibility. That discussion is overdue but beyond the scope of this essay.

In conclusion, let us instead briefly explore the ramifications of the Friedmans' radical policy for developing countries. The Friedmans note that if such privatization of education is to be contemplated, then there would have to be some safety-net assistance for those "hardship cases," for parents too poor to provide for themselves in this way.[30] That is, in considering the more radical solution of privatization, the Friedmans turned their attention from the *universal* vouchers proposed in 1955 to the possibility of *targeted* vouchers. In developing countries, that would seem to be an important part of the picture. While it appears to be the case that a majority of urban parents show themselves willing and able to pay for their children's education, there is still the problem of the minority who do not, as well as the larger proportion in rural areas. Could there be a role here for targeted vouchers for the poorest of the poor, the hardship cases noted by the Friedmans?

One important observation needs to be made at this juncture. As noted above, we found that the private schools themselves, for a mixture of philanthropic and commercial considerations, frequently provide free or subsidized scholarships for the poorest children—typically between 5 and 20 percent of all places.[31] That is, private school owners recognize the need for "targeted vouchers" and are well placed to administer them. Clearly, however, even these do not reach all of the children, so there may be a place for further targeting of vouchers, public or private, or both, to ensure that all families are able to access private schools.

Certainly, successful attempts at creating targeted vouchers are reported from a range of developing countries. In Colombia, for instance, a targeted voucher system was introduced in 1992. Specifically aimed at providing wider access to private education for poor students, it grew to serve about 100,000 students in nearly 2,000 schools after two years.[32] Moreover, there are gender-selective vouchers in Bangladesh, Pakistan, and Guatemala, where vouchers are supplied exclusively to girls to enable them to attend private schools of their parents' choice.[33]

However, another of the objections against vouchers of which the Friedmans take note may be a problem here: "the possibility of fraud."[34] To overcome this problem, they suggest that "the voucher would have to be spent in an approved school or teaching establishment and could be redeemed for cash only by such schools. That would not prevent all fraud—perhaps in the forms of 'kickbacks' to parents—but it should keep fraud to a tolerable level."[35] Such difficulties may not be so easily overcome in some developing countries. Indeed, the problem of corrupt governments may be one of the reasons why grass-roots privatization is occurring in the first place, and why the radical Friedman solution may be a more attractive option in developing than in developed countries. Elsewhere, I have written about the problem of corruption in Hyderabad, India, where state approval (recognition) must be bought for a bribe, not through complying with state regulations, a phenomenon that appears to be relatively universal in the other countries researched.[36] In work exploring public scholarships for deprived children in Karnataka, India, I have also noted how fraud and corruption bedevil their distribution.[37] Nevertheless, there may be ways around those problems, as suggested by the apparent success of the Colombian and Bangladeshi schemes. If fraud and corruption can be kept to a minimum, then the Friedmans' radical solution of a private education market with targeted vouchers for the most disadvantaged may be the most viable solution to the problem of ensuring "education for all" in developing countries. Such a solution would supplement the thriving private market with targeted vouchers—perhaps a mixture of public and private—so that all children could go to the school of their choice (whether public or private). What the Friedmans tentatively proposed in 1980, rather than the more conservative approach presented in 1955, may be the way forward for developing countries today.

There's a long way to go before such a solution will be widely embraced, however. Writing after his second visit to India, Milton Friedman observed that "there is a deadening uniformity of opinion in India, particularly among economists, about issues of economic policy. . . . It was as if they were repeating a catechism, learned by rote, and believed in as a matter of faith." Friedman went on to say that "this was equally so when the responses were patently contradicted by empirical evidence as when they were supported by the evidence or at least not contradicted."[38] That's an apposite depiction of how many contemporary development experts appear to view an enhanced role for the private sector in education. It remains to be seen whether the emerging empirical evidence will sway the future of education policy.

Notes

1. Milton Friedman and Rose Friedman, *Two Lucky People: Memoirs* (London: University of Chicago Press, 1998), pp. 257, 261.
2. Milton Friedman and Rose Friedman, *Free to Choose* (Harmondsworth: Penguin, 1980).
3. Milton Friedman, "The Role of Government in Education," in *Economics and the Public Interest*, ed. Robert A. Solo (New Brunswick, NJ: Rutgers University Press, 1955), pp. 124–26.
4. Ibid., p. 125.
5. Ibid., p. 126.
6. Friedman and Friedman, *Free to Choose*, p. 197.
7. E. G. West, *Education and the State: A Study in Political Economy*, 3d ed. (1965; Indianapolis: Liberty Fund, 1994), pp. 45, 55, 250, 284.
8. Friedman and Friedman, *Free to Choose*, p. 197.
9. Ibid., p. 196. Emphasis added.
10. Ibid., pp. 196–97.
11. Ibid., p. 197.
12. Ibid.
13. Much of our research is being funded by the John Templeton Foundation.
14. Although we know that we found all government and recognized private schools (because there were government lists with which to find them), there was no way of verifying whether or not all unrecognized private schools were found. So these figures show a *lower bound* on the number of private schools.
15. For further details of this philanthropic provision, see James Tooley and Pauline Dixon, "Is There a Conflict between 'Commercial Gain' and 'Concern for the Poor'? Evidence from Private Schools for the Poor in India and Nigeria," *Economic Affairs* 25 (June 2005): 20–26.
16. Parth Shah, ed., *Friedman on India* (New Delhi: Centre for Civil Society, 2000), pp. 9–10.
17. To read in more depth published findings of our research, consult the website of the E. G. West Centre at http://www.ncl.ac.uk/egwest/index.html.
18. Kevin Watkins, *The Oxfam Education Report* (London: Oxfam Great Britain, 2000). For the same type of argument and conclusions, see also, for example, United Nations, *Human Development Report 2003: Millennium Development Goals: A Compact among Nations to End Human Poverty* (New York and Oxford: Oxford University Press, for UNDP, 2003); and World Bank, *Making Services Work for Poor People: World Development Report 2004* (World Bank/Oxford University Press, 2003).
19. Watkins, pp. 229–30.
20. Ibid., p. 333.
21. Ibid., p. 230. Emphasis added.
22. Ibid.
23. Ibid., p. 230; the United Nations' *Human Development Report 2003* makes precisely the same claim on p. 115.
24. Friedman, "The Role of Government in Education," p. 123.

25. Peri-urban areas are the rural areas surrounding a metropolis.

26. Friedman and Friedman, *Free to Choose*, p. 204.

27. Ibid., pp. 204–5.

28. Ibid., p. 203.

29. Ibid., pp. 203–4.

30. Ibid., pp. 196–97.

31. Tooley and Dixon, "Is There a Conflict?"

32. E. G. West, *Education Vouchers in Practice and Principle: A World Survey*, Human Capital Development and Operations Policy Working Papers, 1996, p. 9. See also E. King, L. Rawlings, M. Gutierrez, C. Pardo, and C. Torres, "Colombia's Targeted Education Voucher Program: Features, Coverage, and Participation," World Bank, Development Economics Research Group, Working Paper on Impact Evaluation of Education Reforms no. 3, 1997.

33. West, *Education Vouchers in Practice and Principle*, p. 3. See also E. M. King and R. Bellew, "Educating Women: Lessons from Experience," in *Women's Education in Developing Countries: Barriers, Benefits and Policy*, ed. Elizabeth M. King and M. Anne Hill (Baltimore, MD: Johns Hopkins University Press, 1993).

34. Friedman and Friedman, *Free to Choose*, p. 199.

35. Ibid., p. 200.

36. James Tooley and Pauline Dixon, "An Inspector Calls: The Regulation of 'Budget' Private Schools in Hyderabad, Andhra Pradesh, India," *International Journal of Educational Development* 25 (2005): 269–85.

37. James Tooley, "Management of Private-Aided Education in Karnataka, India: Lessons from an Enduring Public-Private Partnership," *Educational Management, Administration and Leadership* 33, no. 4 (2005): 465–86.

38. Shah, pp. 23–24.

Epilogue: School Vouchers Turn 50, But the Fight Is Just Beginning

Milton Friedman

Elementary and secondary education is, on one level, an industry like all others, with schools producing a service that is consumed by the nation's children. On another level, elementary and secondary education is unique, an industry on which the whole of society rests. As I wrote in 1955, "A stable and democratic society is impossible without a minimum degree of literacy and knowledge on the part of most citizens and without widespread acceptance of some common set of values." That is why government plays such a major role in schooling. It compels attendance in school. Taxpayers pay the bulk of the costs of schooling. Government owns and operates most of the schools.

Government ownership and operation of schools alter fundamentally the way the industry is organized. Consumers are free to buy the products of most industries from anyone who offers them for sale at prices mutually agreed on. In the process, consumers determine how much is produced and by whom, and producers have an incentive to satisfy their customers. Competitive private industries are organized from the bottom up. They have been responsible for truly remarkable economic growth, improvements in products, and increased efficiency in production.

In elementary and secondary education, government decides what is to be produced and who is to consume the products, generally assigning students to schools by their place of residence. The only recourse for dissatisfied parents is through political channels, changing their residence, or forswearing the government subsidy and

This article appeared in the November 2005 issue of the *American Spectator* under the title "Education, The Next 50 Years" and in the November 2005 issue of the *School Choice Advocate* under the title "School Vouchers Turn 50, But the Fight Is Just Beginning."

paying for their children's schooling twice, once in taxes and once in tuition. Parents of more than 10 percent of all students, who go to private schools or are schooled at home, have adopted this final recourse. In short, this industry is organized from the top down.

Performance differs as much as organization. In sharp contrast to other major industries, there has been little, no, or even negative improvement in the product. Children are taught the way they have been for centuries. Functional literacy is very likely lower now than it was a century ago. And we spend more per student, in real dollars corrected for inflation, than we ever have before and more than any other country does now. Top-down organization works no better in the United States than it did in the Soviet Union or East Germany.

The prescription is clear. Change the organization of elementary and secondary schooling from top-down to bottom-up. Convert to a system in which parents choose the schools their children attend— or, more broadly, the educational services their children receive, whether in a brick-and-mortar school or on DVDs or over the Internet or whatever alternative the ingenuity of man can conceive. Parents would pay for educational services with whatever subsidy they receive from the government plus whatever sum they want to add out of their own resources. Producers would be free to enter or leave the industry and would compete to attract students. As in other industries, such a competitive free market would lead to improvements in quality and reductions in cost.

The problem is how to get from here to there. That is where vouchers come in. They offer a means for a gradual transition from top-down to bottom-up organization. However, not just any voucher program will do. In particular, the kind of voucher programs that have been enacted so far will not. Almost all of them have been limited, directly or indirectly, to low-income families, and some have not permitted parents to add on to the voucher, thereby limiting the tuition that can be charged. They are what I have called charity vouchers, not educational vouchers.

They have served their limited purpose well. The families that receive them have benefited; the educational performance of the voucher schools has been better than that of the government schools from which the voucher students came. And the educational performance of those government schools has improved.

Even if such vouchers were much more widespread than they are now, they could not provide the kind of market needed to stimulate innovative experimentation. It is as if when automobiles or television were in their infancy the government had prohibited charging more than a very low price. One function of the rich is to finance innovation. They bought the initial cars and TVs at high prices and thereby supported production while the cost was being brought down, until what started out as a luxury good for the rich became a necessity for the poor.

An educational voucher of reasonable size, though less than the current government spending per student, that was available to all students regardless of income or race or religion and that did not prohibit add-ons or impose detailed regulations on start-up service providers would end up helping the poor more than a charity voucher—not instantly, but after a brief period as competition did its work. Just as the breakup of the Ma Bell monopoly led to a revolution in communications, a breakup of the school monopoly would lead to a revolution in schooling.

There has been some progress toward charity vouchers but almost none toward educational vouchers. The reason, I believe, is that centralization, bureaucratization, and unionization have enabled teachers' union leaders and educational administrators to gain effective control of government elementary and secondary schools. The union leaders and educational administrators rightly regard extended parental choice through vouchers and tax-funded scholarships as the major threat to their monopolistic control. So far, they have been extremely successful in blocking any significant change in the structure of elementary and secondary education in the United States.

The teachers' unions have used their large income (estimated at more than $1.5 billion—that's billion not million) and large membership to gain a major role in the Democratic Party. Teachers' union delegates have been a significant fraction of all delegates to Democratic political conventions. They have made opposition to vouchers a key plank in the party's platform. The unions also have succeeded in persuading most teachers that it is in their self-interest to retain the current dysfunctional system.

Both of those pillars of power rest on shaky ground. The Democratic Party professes, in the words of Sen. Edward Kennedy, "to give voice to the voiceless." But the "voiceless," among whom are surely the residents of low-income areas in big cities, are clearly the main victims of the present schooling system and would be major beneficiaries of a more competitive educational system. Every poll shows them to be strongly in favor of vouchers, yet their political leaders hew to the party line rather than give voice to the educational needs of the voiceless.

Similarly, teachers in government schools, especially the more competent ones, would be among the major beneficiaries of a transition to an educational system dominated by competition and choice. Under the present system, not much more than half of the money spent on government schools goes to teachers in the classroom. The rest goes to administrators, advisers, consultants, and the hoards of nonteaching bureaucrats. In private schools, the bulk of the spending ends up in the classroom. Equally important, teaching conditions are more attractive in private schools, as judged by the higher turnover in government schools despite higher average pay.

Such shaky foundations cannot indefinitely support a system that is so clearly defective, that is inconsistent with the self-image of the Democratic Party, and that is against the self-interest of most teachers in government schools.

I have been saying this for some years now and so far I have been wrong. However, I am not discouraged. Public support for educational vouchers is growing. More and more states are considering proposals for vouchers or tax-funded scholarships. Pressure is building behind each of the 50 dams erected by the special interests. Most major public policy revolutions come only after a lengthy buildup of support. But when the break comes, what had been politically impossible quickly becomes politically inevitable. So it will be for a competitive free-market educational system compatible with our basic values.

About the Contributors

John E. Brandl holds two academic positions. He is a professor in and former dean of the Hubert H. Humphrey Institute of Public Affairs, University of Minnesota, and Distinguished Professor of Public Policy at St. John's University (MN). Some of his previous faculty appointments were at Boston College, Harvard University, the University of Wisconsin, Madison, and the Warsaw School of Economics. Brandl's interests are state government and social and educational policy. He has served as a member of the Minnesota House of Representatives and the Minnesota Senate as well as deputy assistant secretary of the U.S. Department of Health, Education and Welfare, where his primary responsibility was for planning and evaluation of the department's programs in education. Among his awards are the Fordham Foundation Prize for Excellence in Education and the National Governors' Association Award for Distinguished Service to State Government. Brandl has written numerous articles and book chapters as well as *Money and Good Intentions Are Not Enough* (1998). Brandl holds a Ph.D. in economics from Harvard University.

John E. Coons is Professor of Law Emeritus at the University of California, Berkeley; from 1955 to 1967 he was a member of the law faculty at Northwestern University where he began an ongoing series of works on the distribution of resources and authority within school systems in the United States and other Western nations. In the 1970s he served as director of the Childhood and Government Project at Berkeley and was appointed to the National Commission on School Finance by President Carter. Since the 1960s Coons has collaborated in the design of model initiatives and statutory structures calculated to extend choice to ordinary families without imperiling the identity of schools. His most recent essay is "Dodging Democracy: The Educator's Flight from the Specter of School Choice" (*American Journal of Education*, 2005). His first meetings with

Milton Friedman occurred in the mid-1960s when Friedman brought the mysteries of the market to the airwaves as a guest on Coons's radio talk show. As his essay in this volume suggests, Coons still follows Friedman's work with great interest. Coons holds a J.D. from Northwestern University.

Andrew Coulson is the director of the Cato Institute's Center for Educational Freedom. He is the author of the 1999 book *Market Education: The Unknown History* and a contributor to books published by the Fraser Institute and the Hoover Institution, among others. Coulson has written for academic journals, including the *Journal of Research in the Teaching of English* and the *Education Policy Analysis Archives* and for newspapers such as the *Wall Street Journal*, the *Detroit Free Press*, and the *Seattle Times*. He currently serves on the Advisory Council of the E. G. West Centre for Market Solutions in Education at the University of Newcastle, UK. Coulson was a senior fellow in education policy at the Mackinac Center for Public Policy and is editor of *SchoolChoices.org*. Prior to entering the field of education in 1994, he was a systems software engineer with Microsoft Corporation. He holds a BSc. in mathematics and computer science from McGill University.

Jay P. Greene is head of the Department of Education Reform at the University of Arkansas and a senior fellow at the Manhattan Institute. Previously, he was a professor of government at the University of Texas at Austin and the University of Houston. He is the author of *Education Myths* (2005). He has conducted evaluations of school choice and accountability programs in Florida, Charlotte, Milwaukee, Cleveland, and San Antonio. He has also recently published research on high school graduation rates, charter schools, and special education. His research was cited four times in the Supreme Court's opinions in the landmark *Zelman v. Simmons-Harris* case on school vouchers. His articles have appeared in policy journals such as *Public Interest*, *City Journal*, and *Education Next*; in academic journals such as *Georgetown Public Policy Review*, *Education and Urban Society*, and *British Journal of Political Science*, as well as in major newspapers, including the *Wall Street Journal* and the *Washington Post*. Greene earned his Ph.D. from Harvard University.

Eric A. Hanushek is the Paul and Jean Hanna Senior Fellow at the Hoover Institution of Stanford University. He is also chairman of the Executive Committee of the Texas Schools Project at the University of Texas at Dallas, a research associate of the National Bureau of Economic Research, and a member of the Koret Task Force on K–12 Education. A leading expert on educational policy specializing in the economics and finance of schools, Hanushek is a member of the Board of Directors of the National Board for Education Science. His books include *The Economics of Schooling and School Quality* (2003), *Improving America's Schools* (1996), *Making Schools Work* (1994), *Educational Performance of the Poor* (1992), *Improving Information for Social Policy Decisions* (1991), and *Statistical Methods for Social Scientists* (1977). He was also written numerous articles in professional journals. He previously held academic appointments at the University of Rochester, Yale University, and the U.S. Air Force Academy. He has served in government as deputy director of the Congressional Budget Office, senior staff economist at the Council of Economic Advisers, and senior economist at the Cost of Living Council. He is a member of the International Academy of Education and was awarded the Fordham Prize for Distinguished Scholarship in 2004. Hanushek holds a Ph.D. from the Massachusetts Institute of Technology.

Guilbert C. Hentschke is a professor and holder of the Richard T. Cooper and Mary Catherine Cooper Chair in Public School Administration at the University of Southern California's Rossier School of Education where he directs programs on the business of education and teaches courses on emerging educational enterprises and the education industry. Hentschke specializes in strategies for improving educational organizations through business development. Recent publications include *Adventures of Charter School Creators: Leading from the Ground Up* (2004), "Education Management Organizations: Growing a For-Profit Education Industry with Choice, Competition, and Innovation," and "Incentives for Charter Schools: Building School Capacity through Cross-Sectoral Alliances." Hentschke serves on the Boards of Aspen Educational Group, the National Center on Education and the Economy, WestEd Regional Educational Laboratory, the Galaxy Institute for Education, the College-Ready Charter Academy, and Giraffe Charter Schools. His Ph.D. is from Stanford University.

Myron Lieberman is chairman of the Educational Policy Institute, which he cofounded in 1994 to help articulate the case for a free market in education. He has taught at the University of Southern California, the University of Illinois, Oklahoma University, City University of New York, Ohio University, and the University of Pennsylvania. He is the author or coauthor of more than 15 books and a frequent contributor to professional journals and policy publications such as *National Review, Public Interest, Nation,* and *Harper's.* His recent books, *Public Education: An Autopsy* (1995), *The Teacher Unions* (2000), and *Understanding the Teacher Union Contract* (2000), draw on his involvement in a wide range of public education activities. Lieberman is a life member of the National Education Association, a retiree member of the American Federation of Teachers, and a frequent delegate to state and national conventions of those organizations, both of which have commended his leadership in training teacher organization leaders on public policy issues. His experience in collective bargaining includes service as the chief negotiator in more than 200 contracts in school districts in Arizona, Minnesota, California, New Jersey, and New York. Lieberman's forthcoming book, *The Educational Morass* (2006), addresses the role of interest groups, the failure of educational reform, accountability in public and private education, the case for and against vouchers, the educational policies of the Bush administration, and the conflict between supporters of school choice for equity reasons and its supporters for free-market reasons. Lieberman holds a Ph.D. from the University of Illinois.

John Merrifield is a member of the economics faculty at the University of Texas at San Antonio, a position he has held since 1987, and a senior research fellow of the Education Policy Institute and the Fraser Institute. He is the author of *The School Choice Wars* (2001), *School Choices* (2002), and *Parental Choice as an Education Reform Catalyst: Global Lessons* (2005), as well as 37 articles and several chapters in edited books in his primary teaching and research fields of education economics, environmental and natural resource economics, urban and regional economics, and public choice. He earned his Ph.D. in economics from the University of Wyoming,

Abigail Thernstrom is a senior fellow at the Manhattan Institute, a member of the Massachusetts State Board of Education, and vice-chair of the U.S. Commission on Civil Rights. Thernstrom and her husband, Harvard historian Stephan Thernstrom, are the coauthors of *No Excuses: Closing the Racial Gap in Learning* (2003), which was named by both the *Los Angeles Times* and the *American School Board Journal* as one of the best books of 2003. They also collaborated on *America in Black and White: One Nation, Indivisible*, which the *New York Times Book Review*, in its annual end-of-the-year issue, named as one of the notable books of 1997. Thernstrom's 1987 work, *Whose Votes Count? Affirmative Action and Minority Voting Rights*, won four awards, including the American Bar Association's Certificate of Merit and the Anisfield-Wolf prize for the best book on race and ethnicity. It was named the best policy studies book of that year by the Policy Studies Organization and won the Benchmark Book Award from the Center for Judicial Studies. Along with her husband, she also won the 2004 Peter Shaw Memorial Award given by the National Association of Scholars. She serves on the Boards of the Center for Equal Opportunity and the Institute for Justice, among others. From 1992 to 1997 she was a member of the Aspen Institute's Domestic Strategy Group. President Clinton chose Thernstrom as one of three authors to participate in his first "town meeting" on race in Akron, Ohio, in 1997. She earned her Ph.D. from Harvard University.

James Tooley is director of the E. G. West Centre for Market Solutions in Education at the University of Newcastle, UK, where he is also professor of education policy. He was formerly director of education at the Institute of Economic Affairs. Before taking up educational research, he was a mathematics teacher in Zimbabwe. He is the author of *Reclaiming Education* (2000) and *The Global Education Industry* (1999) and coeditor, with David Salisbury, of *What Americans Can Learn from School Choice in Other Countries* (2005). His Ph.D. is from the University of London.

About the Editors

Lenore T. Ealy is president of Thinkitecture, Inc., providing consulting services to leaders in the areas of philanthropy, public policy, and education. Her work in education includes formerly consulting on the development of the Education Industry Leadership Board, a program of the Education Industry Association. Ealy is the founding editor of *Conversations on Philanthropy*, a semiannual journal, published by DonorsTrust, that explores the role of philanthropy in a free society. Other editorial work includes serving as guest editor for the summer 2005 issue of *Economic Affairs* on the theme of philanthropic enterprise. Ealy has served in program and development capacities at a variety of nonprofit educational organizations, including the Heritage Foundation, the Milton and Rose D. Friedman Foundation, and the Intercollegiate Studies Institute. She holds a Ph.D. in the history of moral and political thought from Johns Hopkins University.

Robert C. Enlow has been the executive director of the Milton and Rose D. Friedman Foundation since 2004. He joined the Friedman Foundation when it first opened in 1996, serving as fundraiser, projects coordinator, and vice president before being named executive director. Under his leadership, the Friedman Foundation has become one of the nation's leading advocates of school choice, working in dozens of states to advance school choice by disseminating research, sponsoring seminars, undertaking advertising campaigns, organizing community leaders, and providing grants. Enlow is the author of *Grading Vouchers, Ranking America's School Choice Programs* (2004) and coauthor of "Early School Choice," a chapter in *An Education Agenda: Let Parents Choose Their Children's School* (2001). His articles and quotes have appeared in the *Wall Street Journal*, the *New York Times*, *Arizona Republic,* and *National Review*. He is also a regular guest on talk radio and has testified before the U.S. Senate and legislatures across the country. His civic positions include private sector chairman of the Education Task Force for the American Legislative Exchange Council and Advisory Board member of Children First: School Choice Trust. He holds a BA from Seattle Pacific University.

Index

Africa, 113, 150
African Americans, 28, 31, 36, 42–43, 45–46, 105–6
After-school programs, benefits of, 42–43
Altruism, stimulation of, 28
American Dream, 14
American Education Reform Council, 55
American Federation of Teachers, 82
American Nazis. *See* Nazis, American
Amish, 63
Amistad Academy, 44
Arizona, 75
Asia, 15, 150
Asian Americans, 4, 27, 35–38, 41–42
Aspen Educational Group, 14

Balkanization, 107–8
Bandlaguda, 142
Bangladesh, 151–52
Bhadurpura, 142
Bible Riots of 1844, Philadelphia, 109
Black Rednecks and White Liberals, 42–43
Blaine Amendments, 135
Boston, 40
Boston Globe, 44
Bracey, Gerald, 92
Brookings Institution, 89, 111
Brown v. Board of Education, 39, 72
Busing, 39–41. *See also* Integration, racial

California, 58, 75, 85, 89–90. *See also* Proposition 174
Campbell, David, 110–11
Capitalism and Freedom, 67, 103, 119, 125
Carter, Hodding, 126
Catholics, 53, 75, 109
Center for Education Reform, 131
Chapman, Christopher, 111
Charter schools, 26, 74–77
Chicago, 42, 76
China, 8, 141, 144, 147

Choice, educational vouchers and, 11–33, 35–48, 57–100, 103–19, 125–36, 155–58
California initiative, 89
civic values, 49–56
economic conditions, 20
education levels, 19
for housing, 58
means-tested, 96
Milwaukee voucher plan, 86–100
targeted, 139–54
for vocational education, 20–21
Christianity, 28
Chubb, John E., 85, 89
Civil War, 43–44, 105
Cleveland, 55, 71
Clinton, William, President, 111, 145
Coleman, James, 31
Coleman Report, 99
College Board, 41
Colombia, 151–52
Colombo, Cristoforo, 108
Commission on National Security, 126
Committee for Economic Development, 82
A Common Faith, 28
Communists, 52
Consolidation of school districts, 67–68
Cosby, Bill, 65
Culture, effect on academic achievement, 35–48

Delhi, 147–48
Democratic Education, 49
Denver, 40
Department of Education, 99, 111
Desegregation, 39–41
Dewey, John, 1, 3, 7, 28–33, 60
Discipline, 125–36
District of Columbia, 58, 64, 74–75, 87

Ealy, Lenore T., 1
Early learning, impact of, 14
Economic Policy Institute, 38

Edison schools, 17
Educate, 14
Education and State, 140
Education by Choice, 88–89
Education Commission of the States, 27
Education Week, 98
Education Writers Association, 98
Educational vouchers. *See* Choice
Effective Schools Movement, 30
Elementary and Secondary Education
    Act, 37
Eliot, T. S., 45
Ellison, Ralph, 45
Emergence of inequality, 15–16, 20
Enlow, Robert C., 1
Evolution, teaching, 110

Finn, Chester E. Jr., 90
First Amendment, 61
Florida, 19, 76
Food stamps, 57
Fordham Foundation, 89–90
Franklin, Benjamin, 41
Frederick Douglass Academy, 44
Free Primary Education, 145
Free to Choose, 107, 125, 128, 139
Freedom of choice. *See* Choice
Freud, Sigmund, 45
Friedman
    Milton, 1–8, 10–13, 16–21, 25–26,
        28–29, 35, 40, 49–52, 54–59, 65, 67,
        69–72, 77, 81–89, 92, 103–4, 107–8,
        111, 115–19, 125–36, 139–41, 143,
        145, 148–52, 155–58
        visit to India, 139
    Rose, 2, 81–82, 128, 139–41, 145,
        148–52
Friedman Foundation, 82, 98
Fuller, Howard, 55, 88

Ga, Ghana, 143–45, 147
Gansu Province, China, 143–45
"General Education for Citizenship,"
    50
Georgetown University, 52
Germany, post-Reformation, 110
Ghana, 8, 141, 143, 146, 148, 150
Giammo, Joseph, 53
Great Society, 87
Greece, 108
Greenwald, Rob, 29
Greiveldinger, Deborah, 55
Guatemala, 151
Gutmann, Amy, 4, 49

Harlem, 44
Harvard Graduate School of Education,
    42
Hechinger Institute, 98
Hedges, Larry V., 29
Hemingway, Ernest, 45
Henig, Jeffrey R., 85–86
Heritage Foundation, 89
Hill, Paul, 111
Hirschmann, Albert O., 95
Hispanic population, 4, 27, 35–38, 53
Hodge, Gregory, 44
Homeschooling, 72
Hoover Institution, 89–90
Horace Mann School, 60
Housing vouchers, 58
Hoxby, Caroline, 30–31, 76
Human capital, as engine of wealth, 13
Hyderabad, India, 141–43

"I Have a Dream" speech, by Dr.
    Martin Luther King Jr., 43
India, 8, 113, 116, 141–43, 147–48, 150,
    152
Industrial economy, move to
    knowledge economy, 2
Integration, racial, 54–55
Interdistrict open enrollment, 73–74
Intradistrict open enrollment, 72–73
IQ tests, 148
Islam, 28, 110
Islamic empire, medieval, 110
Italians, 36

James, Estelle, 116
Jefferson, Thomas, 126–27
Jennings, Peter, 145
Judaism, 28
Jurisdiction shopping, 67–68

Kansas City, 64
Kenya, 8, 141, 145, 148, 150
Kerry, John, 46
Keynesian, 103
Kibaki, President, 145
Kibera, Kenya, 143–45
King
    Dr. Martin Luther Jr., 40, 42–43
    Elizabeth M., 116
Kingdon, Geeta Gandhi, 116
KIPP Academy, 44–45
Knowledge economy, move to, 2
Koret Task Force on Education, 89–90
Kozol, Jonathan, 132

Ku Klux Klan, 52

Ladd, Helen, 30
Latin American population, 4, 27, 35–38, 53
Lazy monopoly, urban leaders described as, 96
LeapPads, 14
Lederman, Leon, 126
Leviathan, 59
Levin, David, 44–45
Licensure provisions, for teachers, 42
Little Rock, 40

Macon County, Alabama, 45
Mahbubnagar, 148
Manhattan Institute, 89
Market Education: The Unknown History, 108–10, 112
Marquette University, 55
Marx, Karl, 45
Massachusetts, 44
Means-tested vouchers, 96
Medieval Islamic empire, 110
Mellow, Nicole, 53–54
Michigan, 75, 90
Middle class, defined, 35
Milwaukee voucher plan, 55, 58, 70, 86–100
Minnesota, 26, 74
Missionary teachers, 42
Moe, Terry M., 85, 88–91
Muslims in Hyderabad, 143

NAED. *See* National Assessment of Educational Progress
Nairobi, 144
"A Nation at Risk," 18, 127
National Assessment of Educational Progress, 37–38
National Center for Education Statistics, Department of Education, 111
National Education Association, 64, 82, 103
National Education Longitudinal Study, 54
National Task Force on Minority High Achievement, 41
National Working Commission on School Choice in K–12 Education, 83
Nature of education, changes in, 13–14
Nazis, American, 52

Netherlands, 110
New England, 44
New Haven, 44
New York Times, 98
Niemi, Richard G., 111
Nigeria, 141, 148
Nineteenth-century U.S. subsidized education, 106–7
Nobel, 14
No Child Left Behind Act, 5, 18, 37, 64, 100
Noguera, Pedro, 42–43
North Carolina, 76

Open enrollment
    interdistrict, 73–74
    intradistrict, 72–73
Orfield, Gary, 40
Osborne, Evan, 131
Oxfam Education Report, 145–46

Pakistan, 151
Patterson, Orlando, 43
Pennsylvania, 19
Pilot programs, 132
Polarization of incomes, 15–16, 20
Political tolerance, 52–54
Pragmatism, Dewey as representative of, 29
Princeton, 89
Professional development for teachers, 42–43
Proposition 174, 85, 89
Protestant Bible, 109
Protestantism, 109

Quakers, 109

Racism, 35–48
RAND Corporation, 110
Religious schools, 31–32
Rethinking School Choice, 85
Rickover, Admiral Hyman, 126
Rockoff, Jonah, 76
"The Role of Government in Education," 1, 11, 49, 103–19, 139
Rothstein, Richard, 38–39
Russia, 40

School of Education, 2
Schumpeter, Joseph, 84, 94
Scopes, John, 110
Sectarian Protestantism, 109

Segregation, de jure, 39, 54–55
  racial, 39
Shipler, David, 44
Smith
  Adam, 5, 57
  Kevin, 50
Social capital, as engine of wealth, 13
Social institutions, democratic value
  expression, 3–5, 11–23, 25–65
Sommer, Jack, 9
Sowell, Thomas, 43
Sputnik, 127
St. Augustine, 109
Stanford, 89
Stein, Gertrude, 45
Sub-Saharan Africa, 144
Sugarman, Stephen D., 88–89
Summer school, 42–43
Suryadi, Ace, 116

Targeted vouchers, 139–54
Tax credit programs, 118
Teachers' unions, 1, 70, 81
Television viewing, effect of, 42
Tennessee, 110
Texas, 54, 75–76
Third World, 126
"This Is Freedom; This Is School
  Choice," 59

Tiebout, Charles, 68–69
Tutoring services, Aspen Educational
  Group, 14
Tyranny of the Status Quo, 125

Uganda Railway, 144
Union membership, decline in, 81
Union movement, 81. *See also* Teachers'
  unions
United Kingdom, 106, 115, 140
University of Southern California, 2
University of Texas, 53
U.S. Supreme Court, 39–40, 50–51, 71,
  135

Vedder, Richard, 129
Vespucci, Amerigo, 108
Vocational educational, vouchers for,
  20–21
Vouchers. *See* Choice
Wall Street Journal, 87, 98
Washington Post, 98, 135
Watkins, Kevin, 146
West, E. G., 8, 107, 140
Williams, Polly, 88
Wisconsin, 58
Wolf, Patrick, 52
World Bank, 116, 141, 145

Cato Institute

Founded in 1977, the Cato Institute is a public policy research foundation dedicated to broadening the parameters of policy debate to allow consideration of more options that are consistent with the traditional American principles of limited government, individual liberty, and peace. To that end, the Institute strives to achieve greater involvement of the intelligent, concerned lay public in questions of policy and the proper role of government.

The Institute is named for *Cato's Letters,* libertarian pamphlets that were widely read in the American Colonies in the early 18th century and played a major role in laying the philosophical foundation for the American Revolution.

Despite the achievement of the nation's Founders, today virtually no aspect of life is free from government encroachment. A pervasive intolerance for individual rights is shown by government's arbitrary intrusions into private economic transactions and its disregard for civil liberties.

To counter that trend, the Cato Institute undertakes an extensive publications program that addresses the complete spectrum of policy issues. Books, monographs, and shorter studies are commissioned to examine the federal budget, Social Security, regulation, military spending, international trade, and myriad other issues. Major policy conferences are held throughout the year, from which papers are published thrice yearly in the *Cato Journal.* The Institute also publishes the quarterly magazine *Regulation.*

In order to maintain its independence, the Cato Institute accepts no government funding. Contributions are received from foundations, corporations, and individuals, and other revenue is generated from the sale of publications. The Institute is a nonprofit, tax-exempt, educational foundation under Section 501(c)3 of the Internal Revenue Code.

CATO INSTITUTE
1000 Massachusetts Ave., N.W.
Washington, D.C. 20001
www.cato.org